TOP 10
MALTA & GOZO

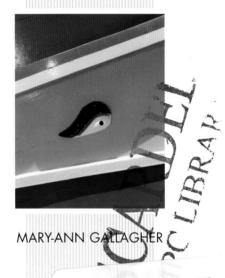

MARY-ANN GALLAGHER

DK
EYEWITNESS TRAVEL

Left **Fish market, Marsaxlokk** Centre **Mnajdra Temple** Right **Historical re-enactment, Valletta**

LONDON, NEW YORK,
MELBOURNE, MUNICH AND DELHI
www.dk.com

Produced by Coppermill Books
55 Salop Road London E17 7HS

Reproduced by Colourscan, Singapore
Printed and bound in China
by Leo Paper Products Ltd

First American Edition, 2007
07 08 09 10 9 8 7 6 5 4 3 2 1

Published in the United States by
DK Publishing, Inc., 375 Hudson Street,
New York, New York 10014

**Copyright 2007 ©
Dorling Kindersley Limited, London
A Penguin Company**

A CIP catalogue record is available from
the British Library.

ISSN 1479-344X
ISBN: 978-0-7566-2491-0

Within each Top 10 list in this book, no hierarchy of
quality or popularity is implied. All 10 are, in the
editor's opinion, of roughly equal merit.

Floors are referred to throughout
in accordance with British usage;
ie the "first floor" is the floor
above ground level.

Contents

Malta's Top 10

The information in this DK Eyewitness Top 10 Travel Guide is checked regularly.
Every effort has been made to ensure that this book is as up-to-date as possible at the time of
going to press. Some details, however, such as telephone numbers, opening hours, prices,
gallery hanging arrangements and travel information are liable to change. The publishers
cannot accept responsibility for any consequences arising from the use of this book, nor for
any material on third party websites, and cannot guarantee that any website address in this
book will be a suitable source of travel information. We value the views and suggestions of
our readers very highly. Please write to: Publisher, DK Eyewitness Travel Guides,
Dorling Kindersley, 80 Strand, London WC2R 0RL.

Left **Golden Bay** Centre **Gobelin Tapestries, Grand Master's Palace** Right **Marina, Vittoriosa**

Left **Blue Lagoon, Comino** Right **Palazzo Parisio, Naxxar**

MALTA'S
TOP 10

MALTA'S TOP 10

TOP 10 Malta and Gozo Highlights

The tiny Maltese archipelago, floating on the cusp of Europe and Africa, has been coveted and invaded throughout its history. The Knights of St John (later of Malta) bequeathed palaces, fortresses and the glorious golden capital Valletta, while the British left red telephone boxes, iced buns and a predilection for tea. It was the islands' earliest settlers who left the most spectacular legacy: the extraordinary megalithic temples, unparalleled elsewhere in the world. Malta, the largest island, has the most cosmopolitan resorts and the edge in cultural treasures, while sleepy Gozo and tiny Comino offer unspoilt countryside and a gentler pace.

1 Grand Master's Palace, Valletta

This is a fittingly splendid home for the supreme head of the Knights. The opulent apartments are filled with treasures ranging from paintings and armour to elaborate friezes *(see pp8–9)*.

2 St John's Co-Cathedral, Valletta

This, one of the world's finest Baroque churches, still belongs to the Knights of Malta. The Oratory contains Caravaggio's masterpiece, *The Beheading of John the Baptist (see pp10–13).*

3 Ħaġar Qim and Mnajdra

These hauntingly beautiful temples made of creamy limestone are set on a wild and rugged cliff-top overlooking the sea. Ħaġar Qim is fascinatingly complex, while Mnajdra's South Temple is the best preserved of all Malta's ancient sites *(see pp14–15)*.

4 Mdina and Rabat

Mdina, Malta's ancient capital, is a magical little city girdled by sturdy walls and filled with medieval palaces and fine churches. Next-door Rabat boasts some of the most important Christian sites in Malta *(see pp16–17)*.

5 Palazzo Parisio, Naxxar

This splendid private palace was utterly transformed by the 6th Marquis of Scicluna in the early years of the 20th century. Its opulent salons and glorious gardens were embellished by the finest craftsman from Malta and Italy *(see pp18–19)*.

Preceding pages Armour of the Knights of St John, in the Armoury of the Grand Master's Palace, Valletta

7 Hal Saflieni Hypogeum, Paola

More than 55 centuries ago, men hewed this extraordinary necropolis out of solid rock. The chambers are spread over three levels and are magnificently carved and decorated *(see pp22–3)*.

6 Marsaxlokk

In this enchanting little fishing village, traditional, brightly painted *luzzus* bob in the blue bay. Maltese families pour in on Sundays to visit the famous fish market on the quays, and then to linger in one of the excellent seafront restaurants *(see pp20–21)*.

8 The Citadel, Rabat/Victoria

The tiny walled Citadel sits high on a lofty promontory right in the centre of Gozo; from this vantage point, views unfold across the entire island and beyond to Malta. Within its walls is a clutch of fascinating museums *(see pp24–5)*.

Malta

ellieha Bay
Mellieha
St Paul's Bay
emxija
St Paul's Islands
Qawra
Bugibba
Ta'Hammud
Bahar-iċ-Ċaghaq
Bur Marrad
Gharghur
Paceville
gare
Victoria Lines
Zebbiegh
Palazzo Parisio 5
Mosta
St Julian's
Sliema
Bingemma
Naxxar
ctoria Lines
Gzira
Valletta 1 2
Mtarfa
Lija
Birkirkara
Attard
Mdina & Rabat 4
Hamrun
Hal Muxi
Senglea
Vittoriosa
Qormi
Paola
Cospicua
Zabbar
Zebbug
Hal-Saflieni Hypogeum 7
Tarxien
Marsaskala
Dingli
Ta'Brija
Luqa
Il-Kappara
Siggiewi
Gudja
Zejtun
Mqabba
Kirkop
Ghaxaq
Hagar Qim & Mnajdra 3
Tas-Bajjada
Qrendi
Safi
Marsaxlokk 6
Il-Biez
Zurrieq
Birzebbuga
Marsaxlokk Bay
3 ├─── miles ┐ 0 ┌ km ───┤ 3
Hal Far
Benghisa

9 Dwejra, Gozo

Gozo's wild, dramatic western coastline is spectacularly beautiful around Dwejra, where the huge Azure Window frames stunning views of the receding cliffs. It's perfect hiking territory, and the diving is among the best in the Med *(see pp26–7)*.

10 Comino

The smallest inhabited island in the Maltese archipelago, tiny Comino is an unspoilt wilderness where the air is still spicily scented with the cumin that gives it its name. You can swim in the Blue Lagoon or hike to spectacular cliffs *(see pp28–9)*.

Note that Malta and Gozo both have towns named Rabat.

⭐Grand Master's Palace, Valletta

This handsome palace was built between 1573 and 1578 by the celebrated Maltese architect Gerolamo Cassar (1520–86), who was also responsible for the Co-Cathedral of St John. Today it is the President's office and seat of the Maltese Parliament, but for more than two hundred years it was the residence of the Grand Master, supreme head of the Order of the Knights of St John. Here, the Grand Master would greet foreign envoys and important guests, and the State Apartments are suitably crammed with reminders of the Order's fabulous wealth and influence. The palace's armoury contains a spectacular array of weaponry and armour spanning more two centuries.

Supreme Council Hall

🕐 The Palace may be closed if Parliament is in session; check with the tourist office in advance.

🍴 There are numerous cafés in the vicinity. Drop into the elegant wine bar Ambrosia *(see p67)* for a delicious light meal.

• Triq Il-Merkanti
• Map J2
• 2124 9349
• Palace: Open 10am–4pm Fri–Wed. Adm Lm2 (concessions Lm1, children 50c)
• Armoury: Open 9am–4:30pm daily. Adm Lm2 (concessions Lm1, children 50c)
• www.heritagemalta.org (armoury only)

Top 10 Features

1. Neptune's Courtyard
2. Corridors of the Knights
3. Tapestry Chamber
4. Gobelin Tapestries
5. Supreme Council Hall
6. Great Siege Frieze
7. Ambassador's Room
8. State Dining Hall
9. Armoury
10. Parade Armour

1 Neptune's Courtyard

The impressive statue that gives its name to the main courtyard *(below)* is attributed to the Flemish-born sculptor Giambologna (1529–1608). It is said that Admiral Andrea Doria, a friend of Grand Master de la Vallette, volunteered to pose naked for the statue.

2 Corridors of the Knights

On the first floor (the *piano nobile*) of the palace, lavishly decorated marble corridors *(main picture)* overlook Neptune's Courtyard. They are lined with portraits of the Grand Masters, their coats of arms and suits of armour.

3 Tapestry Chamber

In this elegant room, the senior Knights attended to day-to-day business and, in later years, the Maltese parliament met. It is now lit dimly to preserve the sumptuous Gobelin tapestries.

4 Gobelin Tapestries

Known as *Les Tentures des Indes* (the Indies Tapestries) *(below)*, for their depictions of exotic scenes, they were donated in 1710 by Grand Master Perellos.

In Jan 2008, Malta abandons the Maltese lira (Lm) and adopts the euro (€). As this book goes to press, Lm1 is equivalent to €2.33.

Great Siege Frieze
This dynamic frieze *(above)* recounting the key events in the Knights' celebrated defence of the island was painted by Matteo Perez d'Aleccio (1547–1616) between 1575 and 1581.

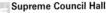

Supreme Council Hall
This is the grandest room in the palace, also known as the Hall of St Michael and St George. It has glittering chandeliers, a coffered ceiling and a stunning frieze *(left)* which vividly depicts the Great Siege of 1565. The minstrel's gallery at one end of the hall once decorated the palace chapel, but came originally from the warship *Grand Carrack* in which the Knights departed from Rhodes.

Ambassador's Room
The Grand Masters used this handsome chamber *(above)* for private audiences and to impress foreign dignitaries. Matteo Perez d'Aleccio painted the frieze, which represents important moments in the history of the Order of St John.

The Maltese Cross

The eight-pointed cross, symbol of the Knights of Malta, can be found throughout the Grand Palace. It is said that the eight points symbolize the eight Beatitudes as well as the eight original *Langues* (national "tongues", or chapters) of the Order. The four arms of the cross are supposed to represent the four cardinal Virtues: Fortitude, Justice, Temperance and Perseverance. Although the cross is traditionally said to date back to the founding of the Order in the 11th century, this particular style of cross didn't come into common use until the mid-16th century.

State Dining Hall
Badly damaged by aerial bombardment during World War II, this beautifully proportioned chamber is lined with portraits of British monarchs and Maltese heads of state.

Armoury
The Palace Armoury *(above)*, located in the former stables, contains more than 5,000 pieces of military hardware. There are cannons, guns and entire walls lined with evil-looking devices for hacking, spearing and spiking your opponent.

Parade Armour
The highlight of the Armoury's collection is exquisitely decorated parade armour made for the Grand Masters. The most elaborate is a suit made for Grand Master Martino Garzes (1595–61), which has an intricate etched pattern.

🔟 St John's Co-Cathedral, Valletta

St John's Co-Cathedral, designed by Gerolamo Cassar and consecrated in 1578, looms over Valletta like a giant fortress. Yet when you step over the threshold, the austerity gives way to an interior of dazzling beauty. The marble floor is covered with richly inlaid tombstones, every wall is intricately carved with flowers and garlands, and the vaulted ceiling is splendidly painted with frescoes by Mattia Preti (1613–99). The Cathedral's treasures include a magnificent painting of St John the Baptist by Caravaggio as well as a series of exquisite tapestries with designs by Rubens and Poussin. Since the 1820s, it has shared cathedral status with Mdina's Cathedral of St Paul.

The choir

⭐ You may be refused entry if you are not dressed respectfully. Shoes with pointed or narrow heels are not allowed as they can damage the delicate floor.

🍴 Nearby you'll find Valletta's most venerable (but pricey) café, the Caffè Cordina (see p66) which has tables out on the square.

• Misraħ San Ġwann (visitors' entrance on Triq Ir-Repubblika)
• Map J2
• 2122 0536
• Open 9:30am–4:30pm Mon–Fri, 9:30am–12:30pm Sat
• Adm Lm2.50

Top 10 Features

1. Façade
2. Cannons
3. Belltowers
4. Nave
5. Marble Tombstones
6. Chapels of the Langues
7. Oratory
8. High Altar
9. Crypt
10. Museum

Façade
The cathedral's severe and unadorned façade is a reminder that it was built as the centrepiece of the new fortress-city of Valletta. Unlike the interior, it was never embellished by later Grand Masters.

Cannons
Two cannons guard the main entrance to the church. They date back to 1600 and 1726; the first bears the Battenburg coat of arms, while the other (above) is engraved with the coat of arms of Grand Master Vilhena (see p36).

Belltowers
The severe belltowers flanking the main entrance (right) are the model for the twin belltowers that adorn virtually every church in Malta.

Nave
The nave (above) was at first as plain as the façade. It was transformed in the 1660s, when Mattia Preti gave it a Baroque makeover and painted his magnificent frescoes depicting episodes from the life of St John.

For more on the Order of the Knights of St John See p13

Marble Tombstones

The entire floor of the church is a sea of multicoloured marble, where 400 Knights are buried beneath dazzling tombstones. Each is adorned with the coat of arms of its aristocratic occupant, along with symbols reminding onlookers of the inevitability of death *(left)*.

Chapels of the Langues

Each of the *Langues* (the national chapters of the Order of St John) was given its own chapel off of one of the aisles on either side of the nave. The *Langues* vied with each other to create the most lavish chapel, and all are richly decorated. Those of Provence and Italy *(above)* are the most sumptuous.

Caravaggio the Knight

When Caravaggio (1571–1610) arrived on Malta in 1607, the celebrated painter had a price on his head; he had killed a man in a street brawl the previous year. In spite of this, he impressed the Grand Master and was made a Knight. But soon after painting *The Beheading of John the Baptist* he was in trouble again; he injured another Knight and was thrown into prison. He escaped, and was stripped of his Knighthood as a "foul and rotten member".

Oratory

The Oratory contains Caravaggio's masterpiece and Malta's most famous work of art, *The Beheading of John the Baptist* (1608).

High Altar

The 17th-century High Altar *(right)* is made of gold, silver and bronze, encrusted with precious jewels in many hues.

Crypt

Here are 12 tombs of Grand Masters, including la Vallette, after whom the city is named, plus that of Sir Oliver Starkey.

Museum

The museum displays the co-cathedral's most important paintings, lavishly embroidered vestments, illuminated antiphonaries, silver plate and a fine collection of 17th-century tapestries.

The crypt is in a poor state of preservation, and is rarely open to the public.

Left **Grim Reaper memorial stone** Centre **Monstrance** Right *The Beheading of John the Baptist*

Treasures of St John's Co-Cathedral

1 Grim Reaper Memorial Stone

Entering the cathedral, you can't miss the chilling depiction of the Grim Reaper, scythe aloft, which adorns the tombstone of a French Knight. The inscription reminds visitors that "You who tread on me will soon be trodden on".

2 Altarpiece of St George

The altarpiece in the Chapel of Aragon was originally Mattia Preti's calling card – he sent it to Malta as an example of his work. It led to his commission to paint the church's ceiling frescoes.

3 Embroidered Vestments

The Cathedral Museum contains ornate robes dating back to the 16th century. Most belonged to the Spanish Grand Master Nicolas Cotoner.

4 Monstrance

This flamboyant Baroque monstrance was made to hold the reliquary containing the right hand of St John the Baptist. Stolen by Napoleon, the reliquary was lost at sea.

Memorial to Nicolas Cotoner

5 The Beheading of John the Baptist (1608)

Caravaggio's emotive masterpiece depicts the very moment after the sword has dropped and St John the Baptist has fallen, bleeding, to the ground.

6 Portraits of the Grand Masters

The highlight of the painting gallery is a series of portraits by the French artist Antoine de Favray (1706–c.1791). The best is his depiction of the pleasure-loving Grand Master Pinto de Fonseca.

7 Tombs of the Grand Masters

The resplendent Chapels of the Langues contain monuments to the Grand Masters. The most lavish belong to Grand Masters Nicolas Cotoner and Ramón Perellos in the Chapel of Aragon.

8 Tapestries

Flemish tapestries, based on cartoons by Rubens and Poussin, are among the most precious objects in the Cathedral Museum. They adorn the church on special occasions, such as the Pope's visit in 1990.

9 Blessed Sacrament Gate

According to legend, this silver gate was painted black to foil Napoleon's rapacious troops. It is one of the few silver objects to survive the plunder.

10 High Altar

The High Altar (1686) is a Baroque design in gilded silver, studded with precious jewels. At the centre, a relief in gilded bronze depicts the Last Supper.

For more on the Grand Masters of the Order of the Knights of St John **See pp36–7**

The Knights of St John

The Order of the Knights of St John was founded in Jerusalem in the 11th century and is the oldest Order of Chivalry in existence. The Knights were required to show proof of noble birth (an ancient rule that was only modified in the 1990s) and were organized into national chapters called Langues. The supreme head is the Grand Master. After the fall of Jerusalem in the late 13th century, the Knights built an island fortress on Rhodes. In 1480, Grand Master Pierre d'Aubusson successfully defended Rhodes against an Ottoman siege. The Knights were, however, ousted by the Ottomans in 1522.

The Holy Roman Emperor Charles V offered the Knights the Maltese islands in exchange for the annual payment of a live Maltese falcon, and they arrived in Malta in 1530. They withstood the Turks during the Great Siege of 1565, built the walled city of Valletta and erected defences across the islands. During the 17th and 18th centuries, as the Ottoman threat diminished, the Order fell into decline. When Napoleon arrived on Maltese shores in 1798, the Knights submitted to the French without a fight. They were forced to leave Malta, but the Order refused to be crushed. Although still stateless today, it continues to function, focusing primarily on charitable and religious works.

Top 10 Important Dates for the Knights of St John

1. c.1100: Order founded after First Crusade.
2. 1309: Knights take island of Rhodes.
3. 1522: Ottomans oust Knights from Rhodes.
4. 1530: Knights given Malta by Charles V.
5. 1565: Knights victorious against Ottomans in first Great Siege.
6. 1571: Ottomans defeated at Battle of Lepanto.
7. 1578: St John's (later co-cathedral) consecrated.
8. 1660s: Mattia Preti transforms St John's into Baroque masterpiece.
9. 1792: Revolutionaries seize the Order's considerable French assets.
10. 1798: Knights cede Malta to Napoleon.

The First Grand Master

This coloured engraving from Father Helyot's *History and Costumes of Monastic Orders* (1842) shows Raymond de Puy, the first Grand Master. His robe is adorned with the white Maltese cross.

The Ottoman siege of Rhodes in 1480

For more on the Maltese Cross See p9

TOP 10 Ħaġar Qim and Mnajdra Temples

These ancient temples of creamy limestone, built during the Ġgantija and Tarxien eras (3600–3200 and 3150–2500 BC respectively), are set on a cliff-top in one of the most beautiful and unspoilt regions of Malta. Ħaġar Qim, unique and complex in design, is also remarkable for its beautiful recovered artifacts. Mnajdra, closer to the cliff-edge, is even more spectacular, particularly in spring surrounded by fields of scarlet poppies. Mnajdra's extraordinary astronomical alignments have led to it being called "a calendar in stone".

Gigantic Stone, Ħaġar Qim

🕐 Special trips are organized by Heritage Malta four times a year (on the solstices and equinoxes) to see the sun's light strike the individual stones in Mnajdra. Book early as there's a very long waiting list.

🍴 The only option for refreshments here is the simple café by the car park.

• Triq Ħaġar Qim, beyond Qrendi
• Map C6
• 2142 4231
• Open daily 9am–4:30pm
• Adm Lm2 (single temple), Lm3 (both temples) (students Lm1, Lm2; children 5–12 yrs 50c, Lm1)
• www.heritagemalta.org

Top 10 Features

1 Main Entrance, Ħaġar Qim
2 Decorative Objects, Ħaġar Qim
3 Gigantic Stone, Ħaġar Qim
4 External Altar, Ħaġar Qim
5 Misqa Tanks
6 Small Temple, Mnajdra
7 Façade of South Temple, Mnajdra
8 Porthole Niche, South Temple, Mnajdra
9 Carving of Temple Façade, Central Temple, Mnajdra
10 Islet of Filfla

2 Decorative Objects, Ħaġar Qim

The most beautiful object found at Ħaġar Qim is the "Venus of Malta", a fertility goddess statue. It is also notable for a pair of finely decorated stone altars, unique in Malta, with an elaborate pitted design.

3 Gigantic Stone, Ħaġar Qim

The biggest stone in the complex – technically called an "orthostat" – is just to the right of the main entrance. It measures a huge 21 sq m (220 sq ft) and weighs 20 tonnes – one of the largest found in any Maltese temple.

1 Main Entrance, Ħaġar Qim

Ħaġar Qim's dramatic main entrance *(below)* remains surprisingly intact, its large honey-coloured stones neatly interlocking.

4 External Altar, Ħaġar Qim

Just beyond the gigantic stone is an exterior shrine and oracle hole *(left)*. It has been suggested that the central column and tapered block are male and female fertility symbols.

5 Misqa Tanks

As you walk from Ħaġar Qim to Mnajdra, you pass a small rocky plateau on the brow of the hill. It is pocked with bell-shaped water tanks, probably carved out of the rock in order to provide the nearby temples with water.

 The "Venus of Malta" and many other key artifacts are held at the National Museum of Archaeology, Valletta **See p40**

Mnajdra

6 Small Temple, Mnajdra

Almost nothing survives of Mnajdra's oldest temple *(above)*, which dates from the Ġgantija era *(see p35)*. It is one of the oldest free-standing monuments in the world, but there is little to see besides some stones with pitted decoration.

Ħaġar Qim

7 Façade of South Temple, Mnajdra

The South Temple is the best preserved in all Malta. The façade *(below)* has a long exterior bench, which suggests that outdoor rituals took place in the courtyard in front.

9 Carving of Temple Façade, Central Temple, Mnajdra

The most recent of the three, the Central Temple was built between the two existing temples. One of its huge orthostats shows a carved representation of a temple façade *(below)* – perhaps an early architectural plan.

10 Islet of Filfla

This tiny offshore islet *(above)* is now a wildlife reserve, but it retains its ancient mystique. It may have had special ritual significance for the temple-builders.

8 Porthole Niche, South Temple, Mnajdra

The porthole niche is one of the finest pieces of original stonework still in situ in Malta's temples. It is framed by three stones with pitted designs.

A Stone Calendar

Mnajdra's South Temple displays an extraordinary astronomical alignment. At the equinoxes (21 Mar and 23 Sep), sunlight shines directly through the main doorway. At the summer solstice (21 Jun), the rays fall on the big stone to the left of the doorway, at the winter solstice (22 Dec), on the corresponding right-hand stone.

For more Maltese temples and ancient sites **See pp34–5**

Mdina and Rabat

Mdina is Malta's most hauntingly beautiful city. It and neighbouring Rabat were once part of the same settlement, but the Arabs walled off Mdina and made it a fortress-city. Still caught within the impregnable walls, it has barely changed in centuries, and the elegant palaces are still home to ancient Maltese families. Mdina remains a tiny time capsule of a city, but Rabat, which spreads beyond the old walls, has developed into a more workaday town. Nonetheless, it boasts some important Christian sights, from the cave where St Paul is said to have lived to early Christian catacombs and mesmerizing medieval frescoes.

Mdina

🎧 A fascinating audio guide is available at St Paul's Catacombs.

☕ Visit the Fontanella Tea Rooms *(see p89)* for a restorative coffee and delicious cakes.

- Map C4
- St Paul's Cathedral: Pjazza San Pawl. 2145 4136. Open Mon–Sat. Free
- Cathedral Museum: Pjazza Ta' L-Arcisqof. 2145 4697. Open Mon–Sat. Adm Lm1
- Palazzo Vilhena: Pjazza San Publiju. 2145 5951. Open daily. Adm Lm1
- Mdina Experience: Pjazza Mesquita. 2145 4322. Open Mon–Sat. Adm Lm2
- Roman Domus: Il-Wesgha Tal-Mużew. 2145 4125. Open daily. Adm Lm2.50
- St Paul's Church: Misrah Il-Parocca. Open Mon–Sat. Free
- St Paul's Catacombs: Triq Sant'Agata. 2145 4526. Open daily. Adm Lm2
- St Agatha's Catacombs: Triq Sant Agata. 2145 4419. Open Mon–Sat. Adm Lm1

Top 10 Features

1. St Paul's Cathedral, Mdina
2. Cathedral Museum, Mdina
3. Palazzo Vilhena, Mdina
4. Triq Villegaignon, Mdina
5. Walls and Gates, Mdina
6. Mdina Experience
7. Roman Domus, Rabat
8. St Paul's Church and Grotto, Rabat
9. St Paul's Catacombs, Rabat
10. St Agatha's Catacombs, Rabat

1 St Paul's Cathedral, Mdina

Lorenzo Gafa's handsome Baroque cathedral *(above)* is topped by an elegant dome. The marble tombstones laid into the floor are dedicated to notable prelates.

2 Cathedral Museum, Mdina

Housed in a faded Baroque building with a sweeping marble staircase, the museum is charming, quirky and old-fashioned. The highlight is a series of Dürer woodcuts.

3 Palazzo Vilhena, Mdina

Grand Master Vilhena commissioned Guion de Mondion, architect of the Manoel Theatre, to build this lavish Baroque palace in 1725. Most of its opulent decoration was stripped away in later years, when it became a hospital. The building now houses a rather dull Natural History Museum *(left)* in the old wards.

St Paul's Cathedral shares "Co-Cathedral" status with St John's, Valletta.

4 Triq Villegaignon, Mdina

Mdina's main street *(left)* is lined with the city's oldest and most beautiful palaces, many of them still occupied by noble families. The finest is the Palazzo Falzon (Norman House), partly from the 13th century and now an excellent museum.

5 Walls and Gates, Mdina

Mdina's lavish, Baroque main gate *(left)* was constructed in 1724. A smaller gate, the Greek Gate, was named after a tiny Greek community that lived nearby. The imposing city walls were first built by the Arabs.

8 St Paul's Church and Grotto, Rabat

St Paul is said to have lived in this grotto during his stay in Malta, and the cave remains a place of pilgrimage. The church *(below)* that protects the grotto is gloomy and dull, but it contains a statue of the Madonna said to have miraculous powers.

6 Mdina Experience

Mdina has numerous audiovisual attractions, of which this is probably the best. It offers a good whistle-stop introduction to the city's history.

7 Roman Domus, Rabat

On the outskirts of Rabat, near Mdina's Greek Gate, this consists of a small museum and the time-worn ruins of an opulent Roman town house. The museum contains some wonderful mosaics and sculptures *(left)*.

St Agatha

St Paul is the most important saint in Malta, but St Agatha comes a close second. According to legend, the beautiful young virgin Agatha, a native of Sicily, caught the eye of the Roman governor but refused his advances. She fled to Malta to escape persecution. She is said to have prayed in a small cave in Rabat, and an underground chapel was later built there in her memory. After a few months (some say years) she returned to Sicily and was then captured by the Roman governor, who had her tortured and killed.

9 St Paul's Catacombs, Rabat

These fascinating Phoenician catacombs, a handful of which have their original decoration, were later used by early Christians.

10 St Agatha's Catacombs, Rabat

St Agatha is said to have prayed here. The main chapel *(left)* is beautifully decorated with medieval frescoes. Half-lost within the catacombs is another, exquisitely painted chapel from the 4th century AD.

Malta's Top 10

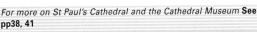

For more on St Paul's Cathedral and the Cathedral Museum **See pp38, 41**

Map of Mdina showing PIAZZA TAS-SUR, IL-WESGHA TA'SANT'AGATA, PIAZZA SAN PAWL, PIAZZA TA L'ARCISQOF, TRIQ VILLEGAIGNON, Greek Gate, Mdina, TRIQ INGUANEZ, PIAZZA SAN PUBLIJU, Main Gate, TRIQ IL-MTAHLEB, PIAZZA SAQQAJJA, Rabat, 500m (550 yards)

Palazzo Parisio, Naxxar

The Palazzo Parisio was originally built in 1733 for Portuguese Grand Master Manoel de Vilhena. In 1898 it was bought by the Marquis Giuseppe Scicluna, who transformed it into one of the island's most extravagantly beautiful residences. The Marquis commissioned the finest Maltese and Italian craftsmen to embellish his palace, filled it with exquisite furnishings and works of art, and introduced modern amenities such as electric light and telephones (Malta's first). Sadly, the Marquis died only a year after the palace's transformation was complete. It remains in the hands of the Scicluna family and the house, along with its glorious Baroque gardens, are now open to the public.

The Music Room

🟢 If you aren't in the mood to explore the palace, it's possible to purchase a ticket just for the gardens.

🟢 The palace's café is perfect for a coffee break or lunch; book in advance for a table out in the sublime gardens.

- Pjazza Vittorja, Naxxar
- Map C4
- 2141 2461
- Open 9am–4pm Mon–Fri (last tour 3pm)
- Adm Lm3.50 (Senior citizens Lm2.50, students Lm2.25, children 5–15 Lm1.75, under-5s free). Gardens only: Lm2.25 (students Lm1.75)
- Adm exclusively by guided tour; tours every hour
- www.palazzoparisio.com

Top 10 Features

1. Façade
2. Entrance Hall
3. Marble Staircase
4. Dining Room
5. Main Bedroom
6. Study/Library
7. Music Room
8. Ballroom
9. Billiard Room
10. Gardens

Façade
The elegant façade of the palace *(below)* is sadly hard to appreciate since it fronts a main road. It overlooks Naxxar's central square, dominated by a flamboyant Baroque church.

Entrance Hall
Opulence envelops you as soon as you enter. The vestibule is flamboyantly decorated in the Pompeii Style with classical statues and a frescoed ceiling.

Marble Staircase
The coping over the magnificent staircase *(right)* is formed by a single piece of gleaming white Carrara marble 6 m (20 ft) in length.

Dining Room
The dining room *(above)* is decorated in the Pompeii Style popular around 1900. The huge dining table is laid with special Royal Doulton china and glittering crystal.

There's another Palazzo Parisio in Valletta; it achieved notoriety as Napoleon's headquarters during his brief visit in 1798 See p33

5 Main Bedroom

Sumptuously decorated in pale green and gold, the bedroom *(right)* boasts hand-painted walls topped with a delicate fringe of green and gold made of stucco. Off the bedroom is a pretty, pastel-hued ladies' dressing room with gilded furniture.

6 Study/Library

With its brocaded curtains and Art Nouveau chairs, this room *(below)* has a decidedly French feel. Stucco reliefs show plump cherubs equipped with a telephone.

7 Music Room

This beautiful little salon has walls of fine silk and an extravagantly gilded ceiling. Each item of furniture features a different musical instrument. The Maltese cross has been incorporated into the design of the inlaid floor.

8 Ballroom

The opulent Ballroom *(right)* is a magnificent golden whirl. Vast chandeliers are reflected in enormous gilt mirrors, and the ceiling is covered with elaborate stucco.

9 Billiard Room

This room still contains the original, enormous billiard table sent over from London. The walls and 3D "carved" ceiling are a triumph of *trompe l'oeil*.

10 Gardens

The palace's beautiful gardens are loveliest, and fragrant with orange and lemon blossom, in spring. There are two formal gardens and an Orangerie with a 17th-century grotto.

The Palazzo in the Movies

This opulent stately home is much in demand today as a film and television location. It has doubled as a French château for the 2002 movie *The Count of Monte Cristo*, as a Genoa hotel in the BBC dramatization of *Daniel Deronda* (2002) and as an Italian villa in another BBC television drama, *Byron* (2003).

In Jan 2008, Malta abandons the Maltese lira (Lm) and adopts the euro (€). As this book goes to press, Lm1 is equivalent to €2.33.

🔟 Marsaxlokk

This enchanting fishing village is set around an azure bay. Traditional fishing boats painted in bright colours bob in the harbour, and the quays are spread with brilliantly coloured fishing nets. Life continues much as it has for decades, if not centuries, in this small and tight-knit community, which has somehow survived the daily deluge of tourists without selling its soul. The modern era has left some ugly marks, however: the power station out on Delimara Point blights the view, as does the enormous container port around the headland. For now at least, Marsaxlokk's sleepy charms remain intact.

Delimara Point

🕐 Book early for Sunday lunch, as many Maltese families like to get together in the pretty seafront town for long lunches.

🍽 There are numerous dining options all along the seafront. Try Ir-Rizzu or Is-Sajjied (*see p97*).

• Map F5

Top 10 Features

1 Luzzus
2 Quays
3 Daily Market
4 Sunday Fish Market
5 Church of Our Lady of Pompeii
6 Fish Restaurants
7 "Seasick Summit" Monument
8 St Lucian's Tower
9 Delimara Point
10 St Peter's Pool

Luzzus

These traditional brightly painted boats *(right)* are said to owe their design to the ancient Phoenicians, who first arrived in Malta around 800 BC. The Eye of Osiris, an ancient symbol of protection against evil, is still painted on every prow.

Quays

The picturesque harbour of Marsaxlokk is hemmed in by quays strewn with brilliantly coloured fishing nets of cobalt blue and emerald green. The local fishermen are usually hard at work fixing boats *(above)* or mending nets.

Daily Market

A section of the quays is dedicated to a daily market *(below)*, where all kinds of clothes, souvenirs, CDs and sunglasses are sold. On Sundays, the tourist tat makes way for fresh fish.

4 Sunday Fish Market

Marsaxlokk's fish market (left) is a local legend. Locals and tourists alike come to gawp at the array of fabulous fresh produce on the seafront stalls. If buying fish, look for bright eyes and red gills.

6 Fish Restaurants

Many of the old fishermen's houses that surround the quays (below) have been converted into fish restaurants. A long, lazy seafood lunch after a visit to the fish market is a Sunday tradition.

8 St Lucian's Tower

This squat little fortress (below) guards the headland beyond Marsaxlokk. It was erected by the Knights in 1610 as part of their coastal defences. Now it houses the Malta Centre for Fisheries Sciences (not open to the public).

5 Church of Our Lady of Pompeii

This pretty little church (below) sits just back from the harbour. As in many Maltese churches, it has two clocks – one painted and permanently set at a few moments before the witching hour of midnight to ward off evil spirits.

7 "Seasick Summit" Monument

A monument on the coast road from Marsaxlokk to Birżebbuġa commemorates the historic meeting of Mikhail Gorbachev and George Bush Sr on board a cruiser in Marsaxlokk Bay in 1989; this marked the beginning of the end of the Cold War.

The "Seasick Summit"

In December 1989, Mikhail Gorbachev and George Bush Sr declared an end to the Cold War after two days of talks aboard a cruiser moored in Marsaxlokk Bay. Unfortunately, the summit coincided with some of the worst storms ever to hit the Maltese coast. The flotilla out in the bay was badly battered, and the Press nicknamed the meeting the "Seasick Summit".

9 Delimara Point

This long finger of land sticks into the sea beyond Marsaxlokk harbour. It is is quiet and rural, with tiny bays, fields, wonderful walks – and a power plant.

10 St Peter's Pool

The closest swimming hole to Marsaxlokk, this (left) is hidden away on the eastern side of Delimara Point. Fishing boats will take you there if you don't have your own transport.

⭐10 Ħal-Saflieni Hypogeum, Paola

This vast underground necropolis is quite simply one of the most extraordinary archaeological sites in the world. It was hewn from the rock around 3600 BC, and later expanded by tunnelling yet deeper. The stunning chambers, carved with incredible delicacy and refinement, echo the forms of the above-ground temples found across the islands. Around 7,000 bodies were found here, deposited over a period of a thousand years. This suggests that only certain members of society were eligible for burial here – but, like so much else relating to Malta's prehistoric temple-building culture, there are more questions than answers.

Oracle Chamber

🔲 Book months in advance; only 80 people are allowed to visit the Hypogeum daily and there is a long waiting list. Note that there is no admission for children under six years of age.

🍴 There is nowhere to eat well in Paola. On the main square in front of the church there are several *pastizzi* vendors.

Triq Ic-Cimiterju
• Map E5
• 2180 5019
• Open daily 9am–4pm
• Adm Lm4 (senior citizens, students and children 6–17 Lm2)
• Advance booking essential
• www.heritagemaltashop.com (bookings); www.heritagemalta.com (information)

Top 10 Features
1. Entrance Trilithon
2. Upper Level (3600–3300 BC)
3. Second Level (3300–3000 BC)
4. Third Level (3000–2400 BC)
5. Oracle Chamber
6. Holy of Holies
7. Main Chamber
8. Snake Pit
9. Sleeping Lady
10. Recovered Artifacts

1 Entrance Trilithon
Most of the constructions in the upper level of the Hypogeum were destroyed by builders in the early 1900s. But the entrance doorway, in the typical trilithon form of two large stones supporting a lintel, has survived intact.

2 Upper Level (3600–3300 BC)
The upper level is the oldest section of the Hypogeum and it is apparent that the temple-builders originally enlarged a natural cave. This is the only level of the necropolis in which some ancient bones have been left *in situ*.

3 Second Level (3300–3000 BC)
The most important chambers – and the most accomplished examples of stone-carving and decoration – are found on this level.

The Hypogeum is poorly signposted in Paola. Luckily, the locals are very used to being asked for directions.

Third Level (3000-2400 BC)
The third level *(right)* is reached via a series of uneven steps. It is thought that these chambers were used for storage, as no bones were found. This level was built at around the time that the temple-building civilization came to its mysterious end.

Entrance Trilithon

Oracle Chamber
The red-ochre swirls that decorate the ceiling of this extraordinary chamber are thought to symbolize the Tree of Life. An "oracle hole" carved into the wall allows low-pitched (usually male) voices to reverberate impressively around the chamber.

Holy of Holies
This is easily the most impressive of all the chambers in the Hypogeum, entered through a magnificently carved monumental façade featuring a fine trilithon doorway. This entrance echoes those of temples found above ground, but is here carved into the rock.

Entrance to third level

Main Chamber
A series of recesses are set into the curved walls of the main chamber *(above)*. Their function remains unclear. Perhaps statues were placed here, or perhaps the dead were left here before finally being buried elsewhere.

Snake Pit
Just off the main chamber is a small cavern, which is known as the "snake pit" or "votive pit". It is possible that it was used for holding animals to be used for sacrifice. The famous statue of the *Sleeping Lady* was found here.

Key
- Upper Level
- Second Level
- Third Level

Sleeping Lady
This is the most beautiful of all the statues found in Malta's ancient temples. The enormously plump woman dreams serenely. Perhaps she symbolizes death – or is a priestess in a trance.

Recovered Artifacts
The many artifacts found in the Hypogeum include amulets, figurines and vases. One of the most curious is a headless statue. It was found with two limestone heads, one of which fits perfectly.

The Hypogeum and the Xagħra Circle

The Hypogeum was first excavated in the early 1900s using rudimentary archaeological techniques, and most of the early notes were subsequently lost. The absence of any information from the opening of this unique site was a huge blow to modern archaeologists, but the discovery of the Xagħra Circle in Gozo (another underground necropolis long thought lost) has given them fresh hope. The Xagħra Circle is being carefully excavated and has provided a wealth of new information that improves our understanding of the Hypogeum.

The Hypogeum's function remains mysterious; some eccentrics have contended that it was a control centre for alien spaceships.

🔟 The Citadel, Rabat/Victoria, Gozo

All roads in Gozo lead to Victoria – or Rabat to locals. The Gozitan capital is crowned by the walled Citadel, the hilltop city whose handsome silhouette is visible from almost everywhere on the island. For many years, the island of Gozo was plagued by raiding corsairs and Saracens, who took the people into slavery. Life was so dangerous that, right up until 1673, the population was required by law, for their own safety, to spend every night within the Citadel. Now rather charmingly run down, the Citadel offers magnificent views, a fine cathedral and a clutch of fascinating museums.

The Citadel, Rabat/Victoria

🕐 **The Citadel Card** offers admission to four museums for Lm2. Audio guides can be picked up at the Cathedral ticket office.

🍴 **Ta' Rikardu** *(see p103)* is a popular choice for a snack.

• Map D2
• Cathedral: Pjazza Katidral. 2155 4101. Open Mon–Sat. Free
• Cathedral Museum: Triq Il-Fosos. 2156 4188. Open daily. Adm Lm1.25
• Museum of Archaeology: Triq Bieb L-Imdina. 2155 6144. Open daily. Adm Lm1
• Old Prison: Triq Il-Fosos. 2156 5988. Open daily. Adm Lm1
• Folklore Museum: Triq Bernardo DeOpuo. 2156 2034. Open daily. Adm Lm1
• Natural Science Museum: Triq Il-Kwartier San Martin. 2155 6153. Open daily. Adm Lm1
• Gozo Crafts Centre: Triq Bieb L-Imdina. 2155 6160. Open daily. Free

Top 10 Features

1 Walls
2 Cathedral
3 Cathedral Museum
4 Museum of Archaeology
5 City Gate
6 Folklore Museum
7 Old Prison
8 Norman Ruins
9 Natural Science Museum
10 Gozo Crafts Centre

1 Walls
The Citadel's sturdy walls *(above)* owe their appearance to the Knights, who had them substantially reinforced after their victory over the Turks in 1565. Although the Turkish threat had been quelled, the Knights feared vengeance.

2 Cathedral
The lavish Baroque cathedral *(main image)* was designed by the renowned Lorenzo Gafa and completed in 1716. It is only the latest place of worship on this site; a megalithic temple is thought to have occupied the hilltop 7,000 years ago.

3 Cathedral Museum
The Cathedral Museum *(below)* contains some eccentric items – like the stole of El Salvadorean Archbishop Oscar Romero, assassinated in 1980 while saying mass.

The Citadel's museums are open from 9am–5:15pm. Last admission is at 4:30pm.

Museum of Archaeology
Housed in the elegant Casa Bondi, this museum contains wonderful artifacts from Ġgantija, Xaghra Circle and other Gozitan sites. Look out for the beautiful "shaman's bundle" (above).

City Gate
The main city gate is very plain, punched through the walls in the 1950s to allow the statue of Santa Marija from the Cathedral to pass. The original city gate is a few steps away.

Folklore Museum
Three adjoining period houses host this intriguing museum. Displays of rural Gozitan life include reconstructions of typical homes, a grain mill (below) and tools for various crafts.

Norman Ruins
Much of the northern part of the Citadel consists of ruined houses, walls and streets, which in many cases have been reduced to rubble. Many date back to the 12th century; EU funds are being sought for reconstruction.

Natural Science Museum
This small museum, located in a 17th-century inn, has rather dull exhibits related to Gozo's wildlife (right), geography and geology. Pride of place goes to a fragment of moon rock, which was donated to the Maltese people by US President Richard Nixon.

Old Prison
This was in use from the mid-16th to the 20th centuries. The cells and corridors are still etched with prisoners' graffiti (above), including a rendition of a galley with its oars. As a young man, Grand Master de la Vallette was imprisoned here after a brawl.

Dragut Rias and the Raid of 1551
Gozo, hard to defend and vulnerable to attack, suffered countless raids by pirates and corsairs. The worst occurred in 1551, when legendary corsair Dragut Rias attacked the Citadel and took nearly 6,000 people into slavery – virtually the entire population of the island. A local soldier, Bernardo DeOpuo, found the thought of his wife and daughters being sold into slavery so intolerable that he slit their throats rather than allow their capture. A street in the Citadel is named after him.

Gozo Crafts Centre
A good place to get an overview of local crafts, particularly lace-making and silk, cotton and wool weaving. Cosy woven rugs, sweaters and other items are usually available to buy.

In Jan 2008, Malta abandons the Maltese lira (Lm) and adopts the euro (€). As this book goes to press, Lm1 is equivalent to €2.33.

🔟 Dwejra, Gozo

The western tip of Gozo is savagely beautiful, with wild, wave-battered cliffs, dramatic rock formations and wind-whipped headlands. This stretch of coastline, known as Dwejra, is blessed with celebrated natural landmarks such as Fungus Rock and the stunning Azure Window – possibly the most photographed sight in Gozo. The area is considered one of the finest in the Mediterranean for diving and snorkelling, and the cliffs are etched with walking paths offering panoramic views. In summer the sea is a calm and perfect blue, but in winter huge waves dash dramatically against the cliffs.

Dwejra Point

🕙 Visit at dusk if possible; a Dwejra sunset is unforgettable.

🍴 Bring a picnic to Dwejra – sources of refreshments are limited to the mobile snack vans.

• Map C1

Top 10 Features

1. Dwejra Point
2. Azure Window
3. Inland Sea
4. Fungus Rock
5. Blue Hole
6. Qawra Tower
7. Dwejra Bay
8. Chapel of St Anne
9. Boat Trips
10. Wildlife

1 Dwejra Point

This mighty promontory is the most westerly point of Gozo's dramatic coast. It is pierced by the Azure Window. Daring visitors walk out to the farthest tip for spectacular views – and sheer drops on either side.

4 Fungus Rock

The strange, squat rock *(above)* in Dwejra Bay gets its name from a rare plant, *Cynomorium coccineum*, that still grows copiously there. The Knights prized the "fungus" highly: anyone caught stealing it was sentenced to three years in the galleys. The rock remains out of bounds to this day.

2 Azure Window

This huge arch of rock *(above)* nearly 100 m (328 ft) high is perhaps the most spectacular natural phenomenon in the Maltese islands.

3 Inland Sea

This shallow lagoon *(below)* is a popular spot for a swim, although it's really more of a pond than a "sea". Boats take visitors in through a passage in the rocks.

The area around Dwejra has no sandy beaches but several good sites for swimming, diving and snorkelling **See pp50–51**

Blue Hole
The Blue Hole *(right)* is another remarkable natural phenomenon close to the Azure Window: a chimney, about 10 m (33 ft) wide and 25 m (82 ft) long, which links the open sea with the Inland Sea through an underwater arch. It's an extremely popular dive site.

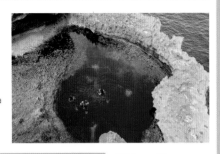

Qawra Tower
This squat little tower *(below)* was erected by the Knights in the 16th century to guard the precious "fungus" that covered Fungus Rock. A hoist was built to winch an official plant-gatherer across to the Rock, which was difficult to scale.

Dwejra Bay
The sweeping bay that curves around Fungus Rock is the best place for swimming as the shallow rocks offer easy access to the water. It's also a popular yacht anchorage.

Chapel of St Anne
This simple little chapel overlooks the Inland Sea. Built in 1963 on the site of a much older church, it is rather dishevelled but important for local people.

Boat Trips
Fishermen run trips *(right)* from the Inland Sea to the Azure Window through a curious rift in the cliff. The journey is short but exhilarating.

Wildlife
Despite illegal hunting and trapping, the Dwejra cliffs remain an important bird breeding and nesting site. As well as the "Malta Fungus", Fungus Rock is home to the rare Maltese wall lizard.

The General's Root
Fungus Rock is known in Maltese as "The General's Rock," after the General of the Galleys who discovered the rank-smelling plant that grows there. The "General's Root," as the plant became known, was thought to cure dysentery, staunch bleeding, and prevent infection in wounds, and the Rock was kept under constant watch to deter thieves. Modern tests have shown the plant to have no medicinal value whatsoever; the Rock is still protected, but purely for reasons of conservation.

Comino

Comino is a diminutive but paradisiacal island with a permanent population of just four or five. The Romans introduced the cumin that gives Comino its name, and its spicy scent, mingled with thyme and other aromatic herbs, lingers headily in the air. It takes just a couple of hours to make a circuit of the island, taking in dramatic cliffs and rocky coves where other visitors – even in the height of summer – rarely penetrate. Comino's most famous natural attraction is the dazzling Blue Lagoon; it's best to stay overnight in the island's one hotel if you want to enjoy its turquoise waters in peace.

St Niklaw Bay

🚤 Boats ferry passengers between Ċirkewwa (on Malta) and Mġarr (on Gozo) all year round; the trip takes around 25 minutes and the standard fare is Lm2. The Comino Hotel *(see p114)* also runs a ferry service for its guests, which non-residents can use for a fee of Lm3.50 per person from March to October..

🍴 The Comino Hotel has a restaurant and there are mobile snack vans, but the best option is to bring a picnic.

• Map A1

Top 10 Features

1. Blue Lagoon
2. St Mary's Tower
3. Chapel of Our Lady's Return from Egypt
4. The Village
5. St Mary's Battery
6. St Niklaw Bay
7. Santa Marija Bay
8. Crystal Lagoon
9. Cominotto
10. Wildlife

Blue Lagoon
This glorious natural inlet *(below)* divides Comino from the miniature islet of Cominotto. Its famously clear azure waters are quiet and sheltered, making them popular with families. The Lagoon has no sandy beach, but the smooth, flat rocks are inviting.

St Mary's Tower
The most imposing building on Comino is a crenellated watchtower guarding the sea passage between Malta and Gozo. It was erected in 1618 by order of Grand Master Alof de Wignacourt, and troops stationed here protected locals against the constant threat of corsair raids.

Chapel of Our Lady's Return from Egypt
This charming chapel *(above)* overlooking Santa Marija Bay is also called the Chapel of the Annunciation. Built in the 13th-century, its simple bell tower and whitewashed walls are reminiscent of Greek island chapels.

The Village
A rather ramshackle building behind St Mary's Tower, this was an isolation hospital in the early 20th century. It houses Comino's few remaining inhabitants.

Comino's single policeman runs up the flag on the little pink police station when he is in residence.

St Mary's Battery
This sturdy battery *(above)* was built by the Knights in 1714 as part of a chain of coastal defences across the Maltese islands. It was topped with a semi-circular gun platform, but the cannons mounted there were never fired.

St Niklaw Bay
This pretty bay is one of only two sandy beaches on Comino, but non-guests at the Comino Hotel must pay a fee to use it.

Santa Marija Bay
Comino's second sandy beach *(above)* is overlooked by a few pink bungalows, a pink police station and a whitewashed chapel. It's perfect for swimming and snorkelling.

Cominotto
Cominotto *(above)*, or Cominetto, is a tiny islet facing Comino across the Blue Lagoon. It has a tiny stretch of beach (at low tide you can wade across from Comino), and its rocky coastline is riddled with numerous caves. It's one of the best diving spots in the area.

Crystal Lagoon
Just beyond the Blue Lagoon, this natural inlet *(below)* is fringed by steep cliffs. As a result it can only be accessed by boat. The incredibly clear waters make it a popular snorkelling site.

Wildlife
Hunting here is illegal, but the ban is regularly violated. In spite of this, Comino offers good bird-watching opportunities, particularly in spring. For such a dry island there is diverse plant life *(left)*.

The Spanish Messiah

The great dream of the Spanish Jew Abraham ben Samuel Abulafia (1240–c.1292) was to create a new religion that would unify Jews, Christians and Muslims. Most people thought he was, at best, insane or, at worst, a heretic. He travelled to Rome, hoping to convert Pope Nicholas III – who died of apoplexy before carrying out his threat to burn Abraham at the stake. After this escape and a spell in Sicily, Abraham withdrew to a cave on the uninhabited island of Comino for three years. He wrote two texts setting out his ideas, but little is known of his later years.

Left **Hagar Qim Temple** Right **"Drinking Doves" mosaic, Roman Domus, Rabat**

🔟 Moments in History

1 Prehistoric Malta (5000 BC–2500 BC)

Human settlement in Malta dates back at least to 5200 BC, although evidence found in the Ghar Dalam cave has raised the possibility that it may have begun as early as 7200 BC. The first of the islands' great temples were built around 3600 BC – a thousand years before the first pyramid in Egypt. The temple period came to an abrupt and mysterious end in 2500 BC.

2 Phoenicians, Carthaginians and Romans (800 BC–AD 4th century)

Little is known of the civilization that occupied the islands from the end of the temple period until the arrival of the Phoenicians in around 800 BC. The Carthaginians used the islands as a military base from the 6th century BC, until their defeat by the Romans in 218 BC. According to legend, St Paul was shipwrecked on Malta in AD 60, initiating the country's long history of religious devotion.

3 Byzantine and Muslim Eras (AD 4th century–1090)

After the division of the Roman Empire in 395, Malta came under the control of the Byzantines until their defeat by the Arab caliphs. The Arabs left their mark both on agriculture and on the language. The islands fell to Count Roger the Norman in 1090.

4 Medieval Malta (1090–1282)

The Maltese enjoyed relative independence under Norman rule, and most continued to practise Islam. In 1194, control of the islands passed to the Swabian kings, who expelled the Muslims for ever. After a brief period of French rule, Malta was acquired by Spain in 1282.

5 Spanish Rule (1282–1530)

Under the Aragonese and later the Castilians, the first local governing body, the Università, was created and the first Maltese nobles were appointed. Charles V gave the islands to the Knights of St John in 1530.

6 Knights of Malta (1530–1798)

The Knights built Valletta, along with many palaces, fortifications, and engineering works like the Wignacourt Aqueduct. They defeated the Turks in the Great Siege of 1565, a fatal blow to Muslim aims in the central Mediterranean.

The Great Siege of 1565

Preceding pages **Sunbathers on the beach at Golden Bay**

7 French Rule (1798–1800)

In 1798, Napoleon took Malta from the Knights without a struggle. He stayed just six days, but stripped the islands bare of all valuables. The outraged Maltese revolted and sought British help. The French were defeated and the British took control.

8 British Rule (1814–1939)

After defeating the French, the British declared Malta a colony in 1814 at the Treaty of Paris. It grew wealthy as an important refuelling station for British steamships on their way to India. In World War I, Malta was used as a vast hospital.

Victory St, Senglea, 4 July 1942

9 World War II (1939–1945)

During World War II, Malta became the most bombed place on earth – 6,700 tons fell in just six weeks. The brave Maltese were awarded the George Cross in 1942 "... to bear witness to a heroism and devotion that will long be famous in history".

10 Post-War Malta (1945–present)

Much of Malta lay in ruins after the war, although the British gave funds for reconstruction. The yearning for independence grew stronger and was finally granted in 1964. In 1979, the last British forces left the islands. Malta joined the EU in 2004.

Top 10 World War II Sites

1 Siege Bell Monument, Valletta

At the tip of Valletta, this huge bell commemorates victims of 1942's Second Great Siege.

2 Unexploded Bomb, Mosta Dome

In the dome is a replica of the bomb that pierced the roof during mass, but miraculously failed to explode (see p38).

3 War Memorial, Floriana

This monument is inscribed with the names of 2,297 British Commonwealth servicemen.

4 George Cross Medal, National War Museum

In 1942, the George Cross was awarded to the Maltese people for their heroism (see p40).

5 Lascaris War Rooms, Valletta

The defence of Malta and the invasion of Sicily were planned in these rooms (see p40).

6 "Faith" biplane, National War Museum

Of three old biplanes, "Faith", "Hope" and "Charity", only Faith survived the war (see p40).

7 Malta At War Museum, Vittoriosa

This interesting little museum has recreated war-time rooms and displays period objects.

8 Red Tower, Marfa Ridge

This 17th-century fortress was used as a signalling station by the British.

9 Luqa airport, Luqa

Malta's airport was an Air Force base; its unusually long runway served supply planes.

10 Dockyard Creek, Vittoriosa

HMS Illustrious, a symbol of bravery to the suffering Maltese, was moored here.

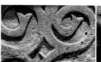

Left **Decorated stones, Tarxien** Centre **Ghar Dalam Cave** Right **Cart ruts, "Clapham Junction"**

🔟 Temples and Ancient Sites

1 Mnajdra, Qrendi

Mnajdra, of all the temples, most captivates visitors, thanks partly to its breathtaking clifftop setting. Its alignment has caused it to be described as a "calendar in stone" (see pp14–15).

2 Ħaġar Qim, Qrendi

Like nearby Mnajdra, Ħaġar Qim sits on a clifftop. A remarkable cache of "Fat Lady" (goddess) figures was found here, plus a fine altar (see pp14–15).

Stone altar, Ħaġar Qim

3 Hal Saflieni Hypogeum, Paola

One of Europe's most extraordinary prehistoric sites, Hal Salflieni is a vast underground burial complex carved from solid rock (see pp22–3).

4 Tarxien Temples, Paola

The largest and one of the latest temple complexes on the islands, this was built between 3000 and 2500 BC. Decorative finds include huge "Fat Ladies" and complex reliefs. An altar containing a flint knife and animal bones suggests that animals were sacrificed at Tarxien. Today the site is unfortunately squeezed by drab suburbs. ◈ Triq It-Tempji Neolitiċi • Map E5 • 2169 5578 • Open daily 9am–5pm • Adm charge • www. heritagemalta.org

5 Ta' Ħaġrat, Mġarr

Two temples form this small complex. The larger, built between 3600 and 3000 BC, is one of the earliest on the islands, while the smaller dates from 3300–3000 BC. The view of Mġarr rising behind the temple ruins is charming. ◈ Triq Ta' Ħaġrat, Mġarr • Map B4 • 2123 9545 • Open Tue 9:30–11am • Adm charge • www. heritagemalta.org

6 Skorba, Żebbiegħ

This small temple complex is, with Ġgantija in Gozo, one of the oldest free-standing monuments in the world. First excavated in the 1960s, the site was undisturbed by earlier, less careful explorations. It was built on an even older village site, and some of the earliest depictions of the human figure, now in Valletta's Museum of Archaeology (see p40), were found here. ◈ Near Mġarr • Map B3 • 2122 2966 • Open Tue 11:30am–1pm • Adm charge • www.heritagemalta.org

Mnajdra

For more on Malta's megalithic temples visit http://web.infinito.it/utenti/m/malta_mega_temples

7 Ġgantija, Xagħra, Gozo

This is one of the best-preserved Neolithic sites on the islands, in a wonderful setting overlooking Gozo's central plateau. The two temples, side-by-side, share the same façade. They were built around 3600 BC.
⊛ Triq Il-Maqdes • Map E1 • 2155 3194 • Open daily 9am–5pm • Adm charge • www.heritagemalta.org

8 Xagħra Circle, Gozo

This underground burial site, undisturbed by earlier excavators, is today providing extraordinary new data. Rare but remarkably well-preserved human remains have been discovered, including a puppy with two children, and a new-born baby in the arms of its mother. ⊛ Map E1 • Not open to public • www.heritagemalta.org

9 "Clapham Junction"

Curious grooves, or "cart ruts", etched into the limestone can be found across Malta. They have never been fully explained, but probably relate to some form of transport. The sheer number of ruts here earned it the nickname "Clapham Junction", after a famously busy London train station (see also p88). ⊛ Near Buskett Woods • Map B5 • 24-hour access • Free • www.heritagemalta.org

10 Għar Dalam Cave and Museum, Birżebbuġa

When Malta was cut off by rising sea levels at the end of the Ice Age, animals adapted to restricted surroundings by evolving smaller forms. The bones of dwarf hippopotamuses and elephants were found here – plus evidence of Malta's earliest human settlement, dating back over 7,000 years. ⊛ Triq Żejtun • Map E6 • 2165 7419 • Open 9am–5pm Mon–Fri • Adm charge • www.heritagemalta.org

Top 10 Archeological Finds

1 "Sleeping Lady"

This exquisite statue of a sleeping woman was carved around 3000 BC. It was found in the Ħal Saflieni Hypogeum.

2 Maltese Venus

Unlike the stylized "Fat Ladies" from many temples, the Maltese Venus of Ħaġar Qim is extraordinarily realistic.

3 Red Skorba Figurines

The earliest representations of the human figure in Malta were a group of small female figurines found at Skorba .

4 Giant Goddess of Tarxien

Perhaps the most striking "Fat Lady", only the lower half of this giant statue survives. A replica is on site at Tarxien.

5 Shaman's Bundle

An intriguing group of pale figurines – human and animal – found at the Xagħra Circle.

6 Snake Relief

A huge stone found at Ġgantija is etched with an undulating snake. Its significance is still a mystery.

7 Bird Pot Sherd

This delicate pot sherd from Ġgantija has a repeating pattern of a crested bird.

8 Animal Friezes

Sheep and pigs, all handsomely carved in relief, strut across a pair of stone apses discovered at Tarxien.

9 Altar Block

This stone altar from Tarxien, with spiral decoration, has a secret compartment where a flint knife and animal bones were found.

10 "The Priest"

This small figurine with a long skirt and a solemn face was found at Tarxien.

The best places to see Malta's archeological finds are the Museums of Archaeology in Valletta and Gozo See pp40–41

Left **Armoury, Grand Master's Palace** Right **Memorial to Jean de Lascaris in St John's Co-Cathedral**

🔟 Grand Masters

1 Phillippe Villier de L'Isle Adam (1521–34)

L'Isle Adam was Grand Master when, in 1522, the Turks defeated the Order of St John and ousted them from Rhodes. The Knights looked for a permanent home for eight years until Charles V of Spain offered them the Maltese islands.

2 Jean Parisot de la Vallette (1557–68)

Brave and charismatic, La Vallette led the Knights in the Great Siege of 1565; he was 70 years old. He responded to Turkish attacks by firing back the heads of Turkish prisoners. After the victory, he began to build the city that bears his name.

3 Jean l'Evêque de la Cassière (1572–81)

La Cassière commissioned the building of St John's in Valletta as the conventual church

Jean l'Evêque de la Cassière

of the Order. (It was granted Co-Cathedral status only in 1816.)

4 Alof de Wignacourt (1601–22)

Wignacourt's term of office was notable for the construction of several coastal fortifications, including the St Lucien Fort at Marsaxlokk and the Wignacourt Tower in St Paul's Bay. He also provided much of the funding for a new aqueduct to bring water from Rabat to Valletta *(see p88)*.

5 Jean de Lascaris Castellar (1636–57)

The Maltese still use the phrase *wiċċ Laskri* (face of Lascaris) for a sour facial expression, after this famously dour man. Like Wignacourt, he commissioned watchtowers and fortifications around the island, such as the Red Tower on Marfa Ridge *(see p80)*.

6 Nicolas Cotoner (1663–80)

Nicolas Cotoner followed his brother Raphael (Grand Master 1660–63). Together, these two Spanish Knights were responsible for the lavish decoration of the interior of St John's Co-Cathedral. Nicolas also strengthened the city walls, and ordered the construction of the Cottonera Lines and Fort Ricasoli, both of which protect the Three Cities *(see pp68–71)*.

7 Antoine Manoel de Vilhena (1722–36)

The Knights generally had as little as possible to do with the locals, but this Portuguese Grand Master was an exception; he did all he could to improve the lives of the Maltese population, and as a result achieved great popularity. He was also responsible for building the suburb of Floriana (just outside Valletta), the exquisite Manoel Theatre, and Fort Manoel in Marsamxett Harbour.

8 Manoel Pinto de Fonseca (1741–73)

This vain, flamboyant and shrewd Grand Master gathered a huge court, which vied with the most fashionable in Europe. Under his rule, many of Valletta's restrained Renaissance buildings were embellished, including the Palace of the Grand Masters and the Auberge de Castille. He died at the age of 92; rumour has it that he owed his longevity to the elixirs concocted by his private alchemist.

Manoel Pinto de Fonseca

9 Ferdinand von Hompesch (1797–9)

Von Hompesch was a mild and well-meaning Grand Master, but entirely unsuited to a stand-off with a cunning and powerful leader such as Napoleon. He oversaw the ignominious cession of Malta to the French, without a single shot being fired. (When Napoleon was defeated at Waterloo, Malta became British.)

10 Andrew Willoughby Ninian Bertie (1988–)

The current – 78th – Grand Master is British. He is primarily responsible for overseeing the Order's charitable activities.

Top 10 Unusual Facts about the Knights

1 Dining off Silver
Invalids in the Knights' Hospital dined off silver plate, for ease of cleaning.

2 Flamboyant Pinto
Among Pinto's staff was a baker whose only job was to make bread for the hounds.

3 English Knight
Sir Oliver Starkey, English secretary to La Vallette, is the only Knight below Grand Master buried in the crypt of St John's.

4 The Maltese Falcon
The Knights paid an annual tribute of a live falcon to the King of Spain – the historical nugget that inspired Dashiell Hammett's celebrated story.

5 Dragut Rais and La Vallette
These heroes on opposing sides during the Great Siege of 1565 had both previously spent time as galley slaves.

6 The Oubliette
Wrongdoers were confined in this dark hole in the rocks beneath Fort St Angelo.

7 Sex and Croquet
To keep his young Knights free of impurity, Grand Master Lascaris made them play *palla a maglio*, a version of croquet.

8 Valletta, Party Capital
By the 18th century, piety forgotten, Valletta was famous for promiscuity and hedonism.

9 Important Relics
When the Knights left Malta in 1798 *(see p13)*, they took the hand of St John the Baptist and other important relics with them.

10 Sovereign Knights of the Order of Malta
The Knights no longer have a permanent home, but claim sovereign (state-like) status.

Malta's Top 10

 The Grand Masters are the supreme leaders of the Order of the Knights of St John (see p13).

Left **St Paul's Cathedral, Mdina** Right **Our Ladies Return from Egypt, Comino**

Churches and Cathedrals

St John's Co-Cathedral, Valletta

St John's Co-Cathedral
One of Valletta's most iconic sights was built as the Knights' conventual church *(see pp10–13)*.

St Paul's Shipwreck Church, Valletta
For many, the arrival of St Paul on the islands in AD 60 is the greatest event in Maltese history. In the depths of this elaborate Baroque church is a fragment of the pillar on which St Paul was beheaded and a venerated relic of the saint's wristbone. Ⓢ *Triq San Pawl • Map J2 • 2122 3348 • Open 9am–noon, Mon–Sat • Free*

Church of St Lawrence, Vittoriosa
Knights and Maltese celebrated the end of the Great Siege here in 1565. Lorenzo Gafa designed the present church in 1681. It was carefully restored after virtual destruction during World War II. Ⓢ *Triq San Lawrenz • Map L5 • 2182 7057 • Open daily 6–9:30am, 4–6pm • Free*

Our Lady of Victories Church, Senglea
The original 18th-century church was destroyed in World War II but has been faithfully restored. The church contains statues of Our Lady of Victories, and of Christ the Redeemer, believed to have healing powers. Ⓢ *Misrah Il-Papa Benedittu XV • Map K6 • 2182 7203 • Open daily for mass from 7am • Free*

St Paul's Cathedral, Mdina
Mdina's cathedral is said to stand on the site of the villa of Roman Governor Publius, converted to Christianity by St Paul. Lorenzo Gafa designed today's elegantly restrained Baroque structure after an earthquake destroyed the original. Ⓢ *Pjazza San Pawl • Map C4 • 2145 4136 • Open 9:30–11:45am, 2–5pm Mon–Fri, 9:30am–4pm Sat • Free*

Mosta Dome, Mosta
Officially Our Lady of the Assumption, this was built from 1833 to 1871. The dome is the third largest in Europe (or perhaps fourth; see Xewkija Church, below). Ⓢ *Pjazza Rotunda • Map C4 • 2143 3826 • Open 9am–11:30pm, 3–5pm Mon–Sat • Free*

Mosta Dome

Catholicism is the state religion in Malta, and 96 per cent of the population are practising Catholics.

7 Ta' Pinu Basilica, Gozo

Thousands of Maltese travel here hoping that Our Lady of Ta' Pinu will cure their ailments. Ex-voto offerings, from crutches to plaster casts, show the strength of their belief. ✪ *Near Gharb on the Ghammar road • Map D1 • 2155 6187 • Open 6:30am–12:15pm, 1:30–7pm Mon–Sat (4:30pm Sun) • Free*

8 Xewkija Church, Gozo

Xewkija Rotunda, completed in 1971, is claimed by Gozitans to have the third largest dome in Europe – but this is disputed by the people of Mosta *(see above)*. The church is big enough to hold three times Xewkija's population. ✪ *St John the Baptist Square • Map E2 • 2155 6793 • Open daily for mass • Free*

Gozo Cathedral nave, Rabat

9 Gozo Cathedral, Rabat/Victoria

Lorenzo Gafa designed this elegant Baroque cathedral, with its wonderful *trompe l'oeil* dome. ✪ *The Citadel • Map D2 • 2155 4101 • Open 9am–4:30pm Mon–Sat • Free*

10 Our Ladies Return from Egypt, Comino

Set back from Santa Marija Bay, this winsome little church dates from the 13th century. The simple whitewashed building is topped with three hooped bells and surrounded by a grove of tamarisk trees. Mass is said twice a week. ✪ *Santa Marija Bay • Map A1 • 2155 6826 • Usually open Sat eve and Sun morning; check in advance • Free*

Top 10 Religious Figures

1 St Paul
In AD 60, St Paul was shipwrecked off the islands; he converted the local populace to Christianity.

2 St Agatha
A patron saint of Malta, St Agatha is said to have hidden from her Roman persecutors in a cave in Rabat.

3 St Publius
Roman Governor Publius was converted to Christianity by St Paul and was appointed first Bishop of Malta.

4 St John the Baptist
St John has been patron saint of the Knights since the Order was founded.

5 Pope Pius V
Pius V helped to pay for the construction of Valletta and sent his best engineers to advise on the project.

6 Our Lady of the Assumption
The most popular incarnation of the Virgin Mary in Malta. Her feast day, on 15 August, is one of the liveliest *festas*.

7 Our Lady of Ta' Pinu
Our Lady of Ta' Pinu is credited with miraculous healing powers *(see left)*.

8 Saint Peter
The feast day of Saints Peter and Paul on 29 June has fused with the traditional Maltese festival of L'Imnarja.

9 San Lawrenz
Unique as the only patron saint to have a Maltese village named after him, in Gozo.

10 St Andrew
Patron saint of fishermen, St Andrew's statue appears in lamp-lit niches across the islands. There's also a statue on the seafront in Xlendi.

Left **National Museum of Fine Arts** Right **National War Museum**

Museums and Arts Centres

1 National Museum of Archaeology, Valletta

A visit is essential to understand fully Malta's unique prehistoric temples. A star attraction is the enigmatic "Sleeping Lady" (about 2000 BC). The lavish salon upstairs gives a glimpse of the building's former glory as the Auberge de Provence. ✆ *Triq Ir-Repubblika • Map H2 • 2122 2163 • Open daily 9am–5pm • Adm charge • www.heritagemalta.org*

2 National Museum of Fine Arts, Valletta

Highlights include works by Mattia Preti (1613–99) and a watercolour of Valletta by the British artist J.M.W. Turner (1775–1851), who never set foot in the islands. There are also delicate sculptures by Antonio Sciortino (1879–1947). ✆ *Admiralty House, Triq Nofs In-Nahr • Map H2 • 2123 3034 • Open 9am–5pm daily • Adm charge*

"Sleeping Lady" – National Museum of Archaeology

3 Museum of St John's Co-Cathedral, Valletta

On display are treasures of the Knights, including vestments, portraits of Grand Masters (look out for Antoine de Favray's rendition of the decadent Pinto), tapestries and the monstrance built to hold the reliquary of the right hand of St John the Baptist. ✆ *Misrah San Ġwann • Map J2 • 2122 0536 • Open 9:30am–4:30pm Mon–Fri; 9:30am–12:30pm Sat • Adm charge*

4 St James Cavalier Centre for Creativity, Valletta

This contemporary arts centre opened in 2000 for the millennium, and is now one of Malta's most dynamic and popular institutions. The emphasis is on events: theatre and film performances, concerts, children's events, workshops, even yoga classes. ✆ *Misrah Kastilja • Map H3 • 2122 3216 • Open 10am–9pm daily • Free • www.sjcav.org*

5 Lascaris War Rooms, Valletta

This fascinating museum is located in the World War II military operation rooms, deep in the bastions of Valletta. An animated commentary vividly evokes Operation Husky (the invasion of Sicily) and other pivotal events planned in these subterranean passages. ✆ *Lascaris Ditch • Map H3 • 2123 4936 • Open 9:30–3pm Mon–Fri, 9:30–12:30 Sat, Sun • Adm charge*

6 National War Museum, Valletta

This small museum, tucked away in a corner, is full of World War II items. There are black-painted Italian torpedo boats, "Faith" (the only surviving biplane of the trio that defended Malta early in the war), and the George Cross awarded to all the Maltese people in 1942. ✆ *Fort St Elmo • Map K1 • 2122 2430 • Open daily 9am–5pm • Adm charge • www.heritagemalta.org*

 Exhibits in Maltese museums are not always well labelled, but curators are generally happy to give explanations to visitors.

7 Malta Maritime Museum, Vittoriosa

Exhibits here range from model ships to lavish ceremonial barges built for the Grand Masters. Look out for the traditional decorations from fishing boats, including a wonderful St George and the dragon. ✎ Xatt Ir-Risq • Map K5 • 2166 0052 • Open daily 9am–5pm • Adm charge • www.heritagemalta.org

Malta Maritime Museum

8 Cathedral Museum, Mdina

The enjoyably diverse collection ranges from worn Roman tombstones to an exquisite 16th-century Hagiothecium (Book of Saints). The highlight is works by the German artist Albrecht Dürer (1471–1528). ✎ Pjazza L'Arċisqof • Map C4 • 2145 4697 • Open 9:30am–4:30pm Mon–Fri, 9:30am–3:30pm Sat • Adm charge

9 Museum of Archaeology, Rabat/Victoria, Gozo

This delightful museum is set in a noble mansion. Ancient Gozitan artifacts are displayed. ✎ Triq Bieb L'Imdina • Map D2 • 2155 6144 • Open daily 9am–5:15pm • Adm charge • www.heritagemalta.org

10 Folklore Museum, Rabat/Victoria, Gozo

This engaging museum occupies three historic houses. Exhibits cover all aspects of rural life in Gozo, with recreations of traditional homes and a display of crafts and trades. ✎ Triq Bernardo DeOpuo • Map D2 • 2156 2034 • Open daily 9am–5:15pm • Adm charge • www.heritagemalta.org

Top 10 Artists and Architects

1 Francesco Buonamici (1490–1562)
This celebrated Italian engineer designed Valletta's first major Baroque buildings.

2 Gerolamo Cassar (1520–92)
Cassar was responsible for the Grand Masters' Palace and St John's Co-Cathedral.

3 Francesco Laparelli da Cortona (1521–71)
The Pope sent Laparelli (once Michelangelo's assistant) to oversee the building of Valletta.

4 Matteo Perez d'Aleccio (1547–1616)
This pupil of Michelangelo created the Great Seige frieze in the Grand Masters' Palace.

5 Tommaso Dingli (1591–66)
Dingli designed Malta's most beautiful Renaissance churches, including St Mary's in Attard.

6 Mattia Preti (1613–99)
Painter of the nave in St John's Co-Cathedral, Preti was perhaps Malta's finest artist.

7 Lorenzo Gafa (1638–1703)
An outstanding Baroque architect, Gafa designed Mdina and Gozo cathedrals.

8 Andrea Belli (1703–22)
Belli remodelled the Auberge de Castille for Grand Master Pinto, adding superb Baroque flourishes.

9 Antoine de Favray (1706–91)
See this French-born artist's portraits and landscapes at the National Museum of Fine Arts.

10 J.M.W. Turner (1775–1851)
Turner painted his renowned watercolour of the Grand Harbour from a postcard.

Left **Blue Lagoon, Comino** Right **Dingli Cliffs**

🔟 Areas of Natural Beauty

1 Dwejra, Gozo
Spectacular cliffs, rocks with supposedly magical powers and curving bays make this stretch of Gozitan coastline among the most scenic regions in the entire Maltese islands *(see pp26–7)*.

2 San Blas Bay, Gozo
This secluded beach can be found at the end of a lush valley filled with fruit trees, and its reddish sand makes a striking contrast with the green of the orchards. There is no direct road for access and just one kiosk in summer, so it is almost always wonderfully peaceful. 🔊 *Map F1*
• *Signposted from Nadur*

3 Ta' Ċenċ Cliffs, Gozo
These sheer, silvery cliffs are hauntingly lovely, particularly at dusk. Wonderful walking trails follow the line of the cliff edge, and the pock-marked limestone landscape is etched with the mysterious Bronze Age "cart ruts".

Ta' Ċenċ Cliffs, Gozo

Dwejra, Gozo

Although illegal hunting remains a problem in the area, these cliffs are home to protected sea and coastal birds, including the blue rock thrush. 🔊 *Map E2*

4 Salt Pans, Gozo
The salt pans are formed by shallow indentations in the creamy limestone, right on the water's edge. In winter storms, the pans fill with sea water, which evaporates in the summer heat to leave behind chunky white crystals of salt. The pools, glassy in winter and oddly pale in summer, have a peculiar yet haunting beauty. 🔊 *Map D1*
• *Between Xwieni Bay and Reqqa Point*

5 Blue Lagoon, Comino
The beautiful Blue Lagoon is formed by a narrow channel which cuts between the small island of Comino and minute Cominetto. The azure waters are shallow and inviting, perfect for swimming, snorkelling and diving. Go out of season if you can, because the Lagoon's languid charms are shattered in summer by the crowds and the motor boats *(see p28)*.

Marfa Ridge

6 This is the wildest and least populated part of the island of Malta. It was historically impossible to defend, which is why few settlements grew up here. The coast is pocked with little bays and beaches (the best are Paradise Bay and Little Armier), and the towering cliffs of Ras Il-Qammieħ rear up at the southwestern end. ✪ Map B2

Fomm Ir-Riħ Bay

7 This wild and remote bay is surrounded by gentle hills with tumbling terraces of pale stone. The only way to get down to the bay is via a steep stone staircase hacked into the rock. As a result it has one of the few beaches in Malta to remain relatively uncrowded in summer. ✪ Map A4

Dingli Cliffs

8 A thrilling road skirts these cliffs, 300 m (1,000 ft) high, which plunge dramatically into the inky sea. This is easily the loveliest and least spoilt corner of Malta, and is particularly beautiful during spring and autumn when the fields are carpeted with wildflowers. Take a picnic of fresh Maltese bread, some pungent local cheese and tomatoes with you. ✪ Map B5

Buskett Gardens

9 In a fairly barren island, the Buskett Gardens stand out as Malta's most extensive woodlands. They were first established as a hunting ground for the Knights, and are filled with groves of olives, citrus trees and plump, bushy pines that look like gigantic broccoli.

Buskett Gardens

Perfect for picnics and leafy walks, these woods are the scene of one of Malta's most enjoyable festivals, L'Imnarja (see p48). ✪ Map C5

Blue Grotto, Wied iż-Żurrieq

10 This huge natural arch in the cliffs near the tiny village of Wied iż-Żurrieq gets its name from the unearthly blue which seems to flicker beneath the waters, evoking thoughts of the mermaids who were believed to live here. A boat trip takes in this and six other caves along the same stretch of coast. ✪ Map D6 • Boats depart from Wied iż-Żurrieq about every 15 mins, 9am–5pm (7pm in high season) daily

Malta's charismatic ex-prime minister Dom Mintoff used to ride his horse down the slippery steps of Fomm Ir-Riħ Bay.

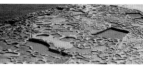

Left **Marfa Ridge** Right **Salt pans near Wied Il-Għasri**

🔟 Walks and Drives

1 Floriana (walk)

Floriana is a town of faded Baroque beauty right at the gates of Valletta. Begin a short tour (1.5 km; 1 mile) by strolling along the Mall, then continue to the Sarria Chapel, decorated by Mattia Preti. Wander through the adjacent Botanic Gardens before visiting the Lion Fountain and turning back towards Valletta. ✎ *Map G3*

2 Circuit of Comino (walk)

This 8-km (5-mile) walk takes a couple of hours. Begin at the Blue Lagoon and take the dirt road to Santa Marija Bay. Follow the curve of the headland (no marked path) to the highest point of Comino. Walk towards St Mary's Battery, then continue around the coast to the Comino Tower and back to the Blue Lagoon. ✎ *Map A1*

3 Victoria Lines: Fomm Ir-Riħ to Baħar iċ-Ċagħaq (walk)

This long, 30-km (19-mile) coast-to-coast hike follows the remnants of the Victoria Lines, British-built fortified walls. Begin at wild Fomm Ir-Riħ (or at Mġarr if relying on public transport), and follow the walls through cliffs and valleys to Baħar iċ-Ċagħaq. ✎ *Map A4*

4 Wied Il-Għasri and Salt Pans, Gozo (walk)

This is a circular 12-km (7-mile) route from Rabat/Victoria. Head for Għasri, then follow the signs for the Wied Il-Għasri, a blaze of colour in spring. Follow the coastline towards Marsalforn to see the salt pans scooped from limestone, and from Marsalforn walk back to Victoria. ✎ *Map D2*

5 Siġġiewi to Dingli (walk)

This walk (10 km; 6 miles) takes in the stunning Dingli Cliffs. Begin in Siġġiewi, pass the pretty chapel of Tal-Providenza, and reach the cliffs at the Underground Chapel. Follow the cliffs to reach the giant golf-ball of Dingli radar station at their highest point. Continue on to Dingli to pick up the bus back. ✎ *Map C5*

6 Delimara Point (walk)

A circular 8-km (5-mile) walk from Marsaxlokk takes in both sides of the point. Make for the bay of Il-Ħofra Żgħira, follow the coast to Peter's Pool for a dip, then to Delimara Point. Return the other side for views of Marsaxlokk Bay. ✎ *Map F5*

Victoria Lines

Comino

7 Xlendi to San Lawrenz, Gozo (walk)

This arduous 12-km (7-mile) walk includes the stunning Dwejra Cliffs. From Xlendi Bay, climb up Tar-Riefnu then continue to Wardija Point. Follow the track to Dwejra Bay, then the path behind the chapel to San Lawrenz. ◈ *Map D2*

8 Marfa Ridge (walk)

A 14-km (9-mile) circuit from Mellieħa Bay takes in all of rugged Marfa Ridge. Head for the Ras il-Qammieħ cliffs, then follow the coast to Ċirkewwa and Aħrax Point, before heading back around the coast to Mellieħa Bay. ◈ *Map A2*

9 North Coast, Gozo (drive)

From Rabat/Victoria, head for pretty Għarb and Ta' Pinu Basilica, then Żebbuġ. Stop in Marsalforn for lunch, then drive east towards Calypso's cave and Ramla Bay to swim before returning via Xagħra to Rabat/Victoria. ◈ *Map D2*

10 West Coast, Malta (drive)

From Qrendi, head for the Ħaġar Qim and Mnajdra temples. Drive on narrow roads to Laferla Cross, then follow signs for the "Clapham Junction" cart ruts and a breathtaking cliff view. Take the cliff road to Dingli. ◈ *Map D6*

Top 10 Viewpoints

1 Upper Barrakka Gardens, Valletta
The beautiful gardens, with their fountains and flowers, frame magnificent views over the stunning Grand Harbour.

2 Dingli Cliffs Viewpoint
At the half-way point on the cliff road along Dingli Cliffs is a spectacular viewpoint. Park and walk to the headland.

3 Red Tower, Marfa Ridge
This squat, crenellated tower high on the ridge offers views over much of Malta and across to Comino and Gozo.

4 Citadel Walls, Rabat/ Victoria, Gozo
Climb to the very top of the ramparts for great views over Gozo's verdant central plain.

5 Xewkija Dome, Gozo
The lift in Xewkija's parish church takes you to the top of the huge dome for spectacular views over all of Gozo.

6 Qammieh Point, Marfa Ridge
From here the massive cliffs of the beautiful, wild coastline stretch in both directions.

7 Dwejra Point, Gozo
Gozo's western coast, with its mighty cliffs and spectacular natural rock formations, looks beautiful from this high point.

8 Mdina's Ramparts
From here you can see major landmarks, including the enormous Mosta Dome.

9 Senglea Tower
This curious tower, in tiny gardens on the tip of Senglea, offers lovely views of Valletta across the Grand Harbour.

10 Wignacourt Tower, St Paul's Bay
This lookout tower, built by the Knights, affords far-reaching views out over the bay.

For more on the "Clapham Common" cart ruts See p35

45

Left **Ramla Bay, Gozo** Right **St Peter's Pool**

Beaches and Resorts

St Peter's Pool, Marsaxlokk

This perfect bay of turquoise water is surrounded by limestone cliffs as pale and creamy as Italian ice cream. The sea is clear and inviting – but watch out for occasional shoals of jellyfish. The pool is a rewarding end to a walk along the Delimara Peninsula, or it can also be reached by fishing boat from Marsaxlokk. ◈ Map F6

Sliema and St Julian's

These are the two major towns within the urban sprawl that stretches northwest of Valletta. The majority of Malta's hotels, restaurants, bars and clubs are concentrated in this area, making it the most popular tourist resort in the Maltese islands. Although there are no sandy beaches, several lidos are dotted along the rocky coast. ◈ Map D4, E4

Sliema and St Julian's

St Paul's Bay

St Paul's Bay

St Paul's Bay is the most attractive of the clutch of resorts that line the shores of the large bay of the same name. Its minuscule port, with its fleet of brightly painted *luzzus*, is still utterly charming. A church is built on the site where St Paul is said to have come ashore after his shipwreck in AD 60. ◈ Map C3

Mellieħa Bay

The sizeable resort town of Mellieħa sits high on a ridge overlooking the sea. At the bottom of the hill is the sweep of golden sand that has made this resort one of the most popular with families. The sand, shallow waters and excellent amenities are perfect for parents with young children. ◈ Map B2

Għajn Tuffieħa Bay and Golden Bay

Two of Malta's most beautiful beaches, these are separated by a wonderful, though challenging, walking path. Golden Bay *(see p82)* is the more accessible and therefore not quite as charming as its little sister. ◈ Map A3

Ramla Bay, Gozo

6 Gozo's prettiest beach, with ochre sands and crystal-clear waters, Ramla Bay is best in the "shoulder" seasons (May–Jun and Sep–Oct), before the crowds arrive or after they have left, yet it's warm enough to swim and picnic. There are a couple of beach cafés and you can strike out along coastal paths in both directions. It is overlooked by Calypso's Cave *(see p100)*, at the end of a short but stiff uphill walk that is rewarded by magnificent views.  *Map E1*

Marsalforn, Gozo

7 Marsalforn is Gozo's largest resort, yet this former fishing village remains enjoyably low-key, and is ideal for a quiet and relaxing holiday. Piled along a ridge on the northern coast, it has all the amenities you would expect, including restaurants, bars and watersports facilities. There's some fine walking along this stretch of coast. Take a stroll to the salt pans *(see p42)*; carved into the limestone, they glimmer beautifully in the sun. *Map E1*

Xlendi, Gozo

8 Xlendi enjoys a dramatic setting, strung out between powerful cliffs and overlooking an attractive bay. Thoughtless development has almost entirely destroyed the village itself, but the scenic backdrop is still more or less intact. Sleepy by the standards of most resorts, Xlendi is Gozo's liveliest holiday town and has all the amenities you would expect. *Map D2*

Blue Lagoon, Comino

9 The dazzling turquoise waters and remote island setting make this the most celebrated beauty spot in all Malta. Although there is no beach as such, the flat rocks around the lagoon fill up in summer with sun-worshippers and families enjoying the shallow, child-friendly waters. The Blue Lagoon is also a great spot for diving and snorkelling, but it's quietest early or late *(see p28)*.

Santa Marija Bay, Comino

Santa Marija Bay, Comino

10 This lovely bay with its sandy beach is overlooked by a charming little pink-painted police station (with a flag to show when the local officer is making his weekly visit). The rugged headland has rocky coves and fine cliff walks. It's very popular in summer, but empties when the day-trippers leave *(see p29)*.

Malta boasts some of the clearest waters in the Mediterranean – just one of the reasons why it's a favourite diving destination.

Left **Carnival** Right **Good Friday celebrations in Mosta**

TOP 10 Festivals and Other Events

1 Carnival
The Knights brought Carnival to Malta in the 16th century. It takes place in the week leading up to Ash Wednesday, and has always been an excuse to let off steam before Lent begins. It is celebrated in villages across the islands with parades, fireworks and fancy dress. The biggest events are in Valletta and Floriana; Nadur, on Gozo, is infamous for its own rather unruly version.

2 Good Friday
Malta is staunchly Catholic, and Good Friday is marked with suitable solemnity. Statues of scenes from the Passion of Christ are paraded through the streets of towns all over the islands.

3 Easter Sunday
In contrast to sombre Good Friday, Easter Sunday is a much more joyful affair. There are more parades, but they include music and sometimes even fireworks. *Figolli* (pastry figures filled with marzipan) are exchanged, along with chocolate eggs and rabbits.

4 Fireworks Festival
The Maltese love fireworks, and every year they show off their prowess using the spectacular Grand Harbour as the theatre. Other countries are invited to participate, and for three consecutive nights the Grand Harbour is ablaze with colour and sound. It's not to be missed if you are in the islands. ◎ *Apr/May*

5 L'Imnarja
One of Malta's most colourful events, this traditional folklore festival is celebrated with music, dance, song and local foods such as *fenkata* ("rabbit feast"). The main arena is Buskett Gardens, where there are bareback horse and donkey races, as well as the traditional singing known as *Ghana*. The carousing carries on all night. ◎ *28/29 Jun*

6 Local Festas
Every village in Malta and Gozo joyfully celebrates the feast day of its patron saint with gaudy lighting and street decorations, brass bands, parades, firework shows, traditional foods and plenty of local wine. The flamboyant parish churches are trimmed with coloured lights, and each village competes to put on the best and wildest *festa*. ◎ *Throughout summer*

Fireworks Festival, Grand Harbour, Valletta

Ash Wednesday falls on 6 Feb in 2008, 25 Feb in 2009, and 17 Feb in 2010; Carnival takes place during the previous week.

7 Jazz Festival
Major international performers are invited to the fabulous three-day jazz festival that is held on the Grand Harbour, Valletta. The setting, just below the massive bastions, is magical, and a variety of musical styles is represented.
⬥ Jul • www.maltajazzfestival.com

8 Malta International Air Show
A great family event, Malta's annual air show displays modern and vintage aircraft which can be explored, plus flying displays. You can see historic aircraft such as Spitfires and Hurricanes in action and enjoy the aerial dexterity of international aerobatic teams.
⬥ Sep • www.maltairshow.com

Historic Cities Festival, Valletta

9 Historic Cities Festival
Every autumn, this ten-day event is held in three historic locations: Mdina, Vittoriosa and Valletta. There are displays of local dance and song and demonstrations of crafts such as glass-blowing and lace-making. Re-enactments of historical events are staged in period costume. ⬥ Oct • www.visitmalta.com

10 Mediterranea
This Gozitan celebration of the arts includes concerts, plays and lectures. There are walks around heritage sites guided by eminent scholars and introductions to local food and wine. ⬥ Oct/Nov
• www.mediterranea.com.mt

Top 10 Festival Traditions

1 Brass Bands
The British introduced this tradition, which has been enthusiastically embraced.

2 Traditional Foods
Local nougat (*qubbajt*) is eaten at all festivals. During L'Imnarja, it's traditional to eat rabbit (*fenek*), and at Easter, marzipan-stuffed pastry *figolli*.

3 Pilgrimages
The devout Maltese make pilgrimages to holy sites such as St Paul's Grotto in Rabat or the Ta' Pinu Basilica in Gozo.

4 Penitents
Penitents follow the floats of Easter processions dressed in pointed hoods. Many are barefoot or carry heavy crosses.

5 Folk Dances
Folk dances are performed in traditional dress. Among them are *il-Maltija* and the *parata*, performed with sticks.

6 Floats
The Maltese take decorations for festivals very seriously. Carnival floats are particularly flamboyant.

7 Confetti
On village feast days, children toss confetti from balconies as the main statue from the church is paraded.

8 Street Decorations
Maltese street decorations are dazzling – literally. Lines of light bulbs outline the church and often the houses too.

9 Fireworks
Fireworks are the soul of every village *festa*; Lija and Mqabba are famous for theirs.

10 Petards
For weeks leading up to the local summer *festas*, children tear around their villages letting off these fire crackers.

Left **Preparing to dive at the Blue Hole, Dwejra, Gozo** Right **Golf at the Royal Malta Golf Club**

🔟 Outdoor Activities

1 Diving and Snorkelling
Maltese waters are renowned for diving and snorkelling. Natural harbours, bays, wrecks, reefs and caves offer endless opportunities for experienced and novice divers alike. The water is warm and clear, and there is a wealth of marine life. Contact the Professional Diving Schools Association for information on dives and schools. ✆ *Msida Court, 61 Msida Sea Front • Map E4 • Info@pdsa.org.mt • www.pdsa.org.mt*

Ghadira Wetland Reserve bird sanctuary

2 Sailing
Malta has a maritime tradition dating back thousands of years, and yachting is very popular. The biggest marinas are to be found in Marsamxett Harbour *(see p106)*.

3 Other Watersports
Most hotels can arrange jet-skis, water-skiing, para-sailing, windsurfing and so on. The best windsurfing areas are Mellieħa and Baħar iċ-Cagħaq. Water polo is a popular spectator sport – in fact, it's a national obsession.

Windsurfing

4 Hiking
Both Malta and Gozo boast excellent hiking trails *(see pp44–5)*; Gozo has the edge because it is much less crowded. Comino is also great for a hike (albeit a short one), if only because few visitors venture beyond the bays. Watch out for Maltese hunters *(see p111)*.

5 Bird-watching
Hunters and trappers have done their best to wipe out the Maltese bird population, but they haven't succeeded yet. They eliminated the Mediterranean peregrine falcon from the beautiful Ta' Ċenċ cliffs, but this area is still home to all kinds of bird life, including the largest colony of breeding Cory's Shearwaters in the Maltese islands. There are two bird sanctuaries in Malta *(see p79)*.

6 Golf
Malta has just one golf course, the Royal Malta Golf Club. It is open to visitors daily except Thursday and Saturday mornings, but advance booking is essential. Facilities include changing rooms, bar, restaurant, pro shop, practice putting green and driving range. Equipment can be hired, and lessons are available for golfers of all abilities. Note that "proper golf attire" (polo shirt, tailored trousers or shorts) is compulsory. ✆ *Triq Aldo Moro, Marsa • Map D4 • 2123 9302 • www.maltagolf.org*

Boat excursion, Crystal Lagoon, Comino

Top 10 Diving and Snorkelling Sites

1 Marfa Point, Ċirkewwa
Good for night dives, with moray eels, octopuses and corals. Has a training pool for beginners. ◈ *Map A2*

2 Ahrax Point
Off Marfa Ridge. Huge seaweed meadows shelter abundant marine life. Good visibility for photos. ◈ *Map B2*

3 Blenheim Bomber, Marsaxlokk
The remains of this World War II plane make for an interesting but difficult dive. ◈ *Map F5*

4 Delimara Point
This site is reached by boat. Groupers and stingrays are often seen. ◈ *Map F6*

5 Fungus Rock, Gozo
Several good sites cluster around Dwejra; this huge rock, covered in marine life, is one of the best. ◈ *Map C1*

6 Azure Window, Gozo
Another scenic dive at Dwejra. Huge boulders shelter abundant marine life. ◈ *Map C1*

7 The Blue Dome, or Cathedral Cave, Gozo
One of the best. Light reflects onto the vast ceiling, creating the "blue dome" effect. Fish include sea horses. ◈ *Map D1*

8 San Dimitri Point, Gozo
Accessible only by boat. There are shoals of barracuda and many other fish. ◈ *Map C1*

9 Lighthouse Reef, Comino
Perhaps Comino's best site, with a chimney through the reef. Marine life includes sea horses and starfish. ◈ *Map A1*

10 Santa Marija Caves, Comino
Several caves, some offering spectacular swim-throughs. A good photo spot. ◈ *Map A1*

7 Boat Excursions
Numerous boat excursions are available, from a tour of the Grand Harbour to jaunts taking in all three main islands. In Malta, most trips start from Sliema, in Gozo from Xlendi Bay.

8 Rock-climbing
There are no mountains, but the cliffs offer exciting challenges for climbers. More than 1,200 established routes include climbs suitable for people of all abilities. Local tour operator Malta Rock Climbing can organise courses and climbing holidays. ◈ *2148 0240* • *Info@malta-rockclimbing.com* • *www.malta-rockclimbing.com*

9 Horse-riding
Malta has a long tradition of horse-riding, and even boasts Europe's oldest polo club. There are numerous stables where you can arrange children's pony rides or longer treks for experienced riders. Malta's Tourism Authority can supply a list of approved centres. ◈ *www.visitmalta.com*

10 Cycling
The volume of traffic, terrible roads and appalling driving make cycling a bad idea on the island of Malta. On Gozo, the surfaces and drivers are just as bad, but the roads are generally very quiet. Be prepared for steep hills.

Left **Malta Experience** Right **Mellieha Bay**

Children's Activities

1 Malta Experience, Valletta
Malta has countless audio-visual attractions, mostly in Valletta and Mdina. This one offers a good introduction to Maltese history on a giant screen, but the 45-minute show may be a bit too long for smaller children.
§ *Mediterranean Conference Centre, Triq Il-Mediterran • Map K2 • 2124 3776 • On the hour 11am–4pm Mon–Fri, 11am–1pm Sat, Sun (2pm Oct–Jun) • Adm charge • www.themaltaexperience.com*

2 Pirate Boat Excursion
The whole family can become pirates for a day on this fun cruise. Activities include walking the plank, a treasure hunt and sword fights staged by the crew. Lunch is included, and there is ample opportunity for swimming and snorkelling. § *Tigné Seafront, Sliema • Map R3 • 2346 3333 • Wed & Sat, end Jun to mid-Sep • Adm charge • www.captainmorgan.com.mt*

3 Mediterraneo Marine Park
This seaside marine park puts on daily shows by dolphins, sea lions and parrots. The reptile room and seal pool are also popular, but for many the highlight is the

Mediterraneo Marine Park

Popeye Village

chance to swim with dolphins (book ahead). § *Bahar Ic-Caghaq • Map D3 • 2137 2218 • Open daily 10am–5pm Apr–Oct (check show times) • Adm charge • www.mediterraneo.com.mt*

4 Splash & Fun Park
You'll find a lagoon-shaped swimming pool with varied chutes and a dinosaur-themed play area for smaller kids. There's a simple café, but it's best to bring snacks. It's very crowded in high season, particularly at weekends. § *Bahar Ic-Caghaq • Map D3 • 2137 4283 • Open daily 9:30–4:30pm • Adm charge*

5 Popeye Village, Anchor Bay
Popeye's home town of Sweethaven was recreated here for *Popeye, the Movie.* Besides the film set, younger children may also enjoy the adjoining fun park. The tiny beach is a good spot for a picnic. § *Map A3 • 2152 4782 • Open daily 9:30am–7pm Apr–Sep; 9:30am–4:30pm Oct–Mar • Adm charge • www.popeyemalta.com*

As in most southern-Mediterranean cultures, the Maltese adore children and will do everything they can to make yours welcome.

Playmobil Park, Hal-Far

Kids aged 6-plus can tour the world's second-largest Playmobil factory and see all their favourite characters being made. There's also a small play park (for children 3 and over), café and shop. ✆ Hal-Far Industrial Estate • Map E6 • 2224 2445 • Open Oct–Jun: 10am–6pm daily; Jul–Sep: 10am–6pm Mon–Sat, 10am–1pm Sun • www.playmobilmalta.com

Malta Aviation Museum

Kids will enjoy seeing the large collection of vintage aircraft on display. The more technically-minded can watch volunteers restoring the planes. ✆ Ta' Qali Aerodrome, between Mdina and Attard • Map C4 • Open daily 9am–5pm • Adm charge • www.maltaaviationmuseum.com

Historical Re-enactments, Forts Elmo and Rinella

Fort Rinella (see p70) shows the world of the Victorian soldier, with signalling displays and weapons fire. Fort Elmo stages full-scale military parades in period costume. ✆ Fort

Historical re-enactments

Elmo, Valletta • Map K1, E4 • 2123 7747 • Check dates with Malta Tourism Authority • Adm charge. • www.visitmalta.com

Hal Saflieni Hypogeum

This underground burial cavern is the most dramatic of Malta's ancient sites, and the best for children – but under-6s are not admitted (see pp22–3).

Mellieħa Bay

This popular, sandy and shallow bay is good for families with small children (see p46).

Top 10 Child-friendly Restaurants

1 The Avenue, Paċeville
A colourful, buzzy budget restaurant (see p75).

2 Henry J. Beans American Bar & Grill, St Julian's
A 1950s-style burger-and-rib joint with an outdoor terrace. ✆ Corinthia San Ġorġ, St George's Bay • 2370 2696

3 Piccolo Padre, St Julian's
A popular Italian restaurant serving great pasta and pizzas. ✆ 194 Main Street • 2134 4875

4 Hard Rock Café, St Julian's
The rock-themed decor features Cher's dress, and the menu the usual burgers and fajitas. ✆ Bay Street Hotel Complex, St George's Bay • 2372 2253

5 Tal-Familja, Marsaskala
This friendly seafood spot is a favourite with Maltese families (see p97).

6 Fontanella Tea Gardens, Mdina
Service may be slow, but kids seem to like these outdoor tea rooms (see p89).

7 Blue Creek, Għar Lapsi
Overlooking the popular lido, this restaurant is very family-friendly (see p97).

8 Tex Mex Grill & Cantina, Sliema
This raucous US-themed spot is always a hit with youngsters. ✆ 132A Triq Il-Torri • 2133 9247

9 Ciao Bella Pizzeria, St Paul's Bay
A rustically furnished Italian trattoria, this is a great family choice (see p83).

10 Oleander, Gozo
This country restaurant serving local cuisine welcomes kids enthusiastically (see p103).

Left **Bread vendor** Centre *Qubbajt* Right *Mqaret*

Culinary Highlights

Maltese Bread
The Maltese are justly proud of their excellent bread. Most villages have at least one bakery, where you can pick up delicious *hobz* (small soft rolls) or *ftira* (a ring-shaped loaf that is similar in texture to Italian *ciabatta*).

Gbejniet
These small round cheeselets are typical of Gozo and are made from goat or sheep's milk. There are two common kinds: the plain, which is smooth and creamy, and the peppered version, which is piquant and perfect with the local crusty bread and a slice of tomato. These cheeses are often used to flavour other dishes, such as soups.

TRADITIONAL SET MENU
Traditional Starters
LOCAL GOAT'S CHEESE SALAD.
VEGETABLE SOUP.
SPAGHETTI WITH RABBIT SAUCE.
Traditional Main Course
FRIED RABBIT IN GARLIC & WHITE WINE.
GRILLED SWORDFISH
CHICKEN IN WHITE WINE & TOMATOES
All main courses are served with vegetables & potatoes.
CHOICE OF COFFEE
Lm 3.75

Traditional menu including rabbit *(fenek)*

Soppa Tal-Armla
Maltese cuisine boasts many delicious soups, including *minestra* (vegetable soup) and the traditional *soppa tal-armla* (literally "widow's soup"). This

Ftira and *gbejniet*

name probably comes from the simple ingredients, which include potatoes, courgettes and other vegetables, plus a dollop of ricotta cheese or a *gbejniet* cheeselet.

Bragioli
Bragioli are "beef olives", similar to the Italian version. They are made using slices of beef or veal stuffed with a mixture of cheese, ham and herbs, then braised gently on the stove or in the oven.

Fenek
Fenek (rabbit) is the most popular meat in Malta, and a favourite for *festas* and special events. It is prepared in countless ways, but the most common include rabbit stew made with wine and flavoured with herbs, roast rabbit served with a bitter chocolate sauce, and a simple dish of spaghetti with a rabbit sauce.

Torta Tal-lampuki
This fish pie is made with *lampuki*, a prized local fish that is only available for a short period each year (usually from September to November). Such is the demand for this fish that rights to catch it are granted by lottery. The pie combines the fish with vegetables, walnuts, olives and raisins, and is considered a great delicacy by locals.

 Gbejniet made with sheep's milk are considered superior in taste to those made with goats' or cows' milk.

Qubbajt

This nougat-style sweet is made with almonds and honey, and is traditionally eaten at festivals and special events. There are always several stalls selling *qubbajt* at village *festas*, but it is also available year-round from stalls and local shops. It is said to date back to the Arab occupation of the islands.

Pastizzi and Qassatat

Pastizzi – Malta's favourite snack – are tasty, diamond-shaped pastry parcels stuffed with ricotta cheese or a pea mixture. *Pastizzi* stalls can be found everywhere, and virtually every old-fashioned bar will offer its own, home-made versions. *Qassatat* are similar to *pastizzi* but made of a lighter pastry and round in shape.

Qassatat

Hobz Biz-zejt

These are chunks of bread brushed with olive oil and topped with a mixture of roughly chopped tomatoes, onions and herbs. They were traditionally considered a humble snack, akin to Italian *crostini*, but have acquired a sophisticated cachet in recent years and are regularly served in smart bars and restaurants as appetizers.

Mqaret

Mqaret are scrumptious pastry parcels, filled with a date mixture and deep-fried. They make the perfect sweet snack, and are delicious, if fattening.

Top 10 Drinks

1 Ċisk Lager

An excellent lager beer, this is very refreshing on burning-hot summer days.

2 Hopleaf Pale Ale

A tasty amber ale that goes well with a couple of *pastizzi*. Like Ċisk, it's made by Farsons.

3 Blue Label Ale

This popular Farsons brew has a sweet, malty taste.

4 Wine

Maltese wine has improved a lot in recent years. The main producers are Marsovin, Delicata and Meridiana.

5 Kinnie

Peculiar to Malta, this is a slightly bitter, fizzy soft drink flavoured with orange and herbs.

6 Anisette

This aniseed-flavoured liqueur is a Gozitan speciality, and is an ingredient in many local pastries and biscuits.

7 Bajtra Liqueur

The fat, stumpy limbs of prickly pear cacti grow all over the islands. The red, ear-like fruits are used in this sweet liqueur, which is also flavoured with honey and herbs.

8 Coffee

Maltese coffee may sound Italian (*cappuccino, espresso*) but lacks the kick. It's served long and milky for breakfast.

9 Tea

The Maltese remain attached to tea, introduced by the British and often, especially in rural areas, very strong.

10 Bottled Water

Much of the tap water in Malta is produced by a "reverse osmosis" process (which converts sea water into drinking water). Most people prefer to drink bottled water, much of it produced locally.

Left **Bacchus, Mdina** Right **Ta' Rikardu, Rabat/Victoria**

Restaurants

1 Giannini, Valletta

A townhouse with beautiful views over Marsamxett Harbour houses perhaps Valletta's best restaurant, with creative Maltese and Italian cuisine. The set menu "A journey through the Maltese Islands" is a good introduction to local cooking. ✆ *23 Triq L-Imitihen • Map H2 • 2123 7121 • Closed Sat L, Sun • €€€€*

2 Rubino, Valletta

One of the best places for traditional Maltese soups and stews. It began as a confectionery shop and is still famous for its desserts; the *cassata Siciliana* – a rich and creamy concoction made with ricotta cheese – is heavenly. ✆ *53 Triq Il-Fran • Map H2 • 2122 4656 • Closed Mon, Wed–Thu D, Aug (open for confectionery only Sun); reservations highly recommended • €€€*

3 Da Pippo, Valletta

This welcoming, rustic-style trattoria is regularly voted as Valletta's best budget restaurant. All the food is fresh, home-cooked and surprisingly affordable. Go for the superb fresh fish, which is selected daily from the local catch. ✆ *136 Triq Melita • Map H2 • 2124 8029 • Open for lunch only; advance booking essential; closed Sun • €€*

4 Ta' Frenc, Marsalforn, Gozo

Housed in an exquisitely restored 14th-century farmhouse, the sublime Ta' Frenc features excellent Maltese and Mediterranean cuisine, with many ingredients from its own farm. Try fresh local fish baked in an anise-flavoured salt crust, or hand-made seafood ravioli. ✆ *Triq Ghajn Damma (off Marsalforn Road) • Map E1 • 2155 3888 • Closed Jan–Feb Mon–Thu L & D, Fri & Sat L, Sun D; Tue all year • €€€€*

5 Jeffrey's, Għarb, Gozo

A friendly, simple restaurant in an old farmhouse, this has a lovely ivy-draped courtyard. Choose from traditional dishes such as rabbit stew (the speciality) or fresh local fish. ✆ *10 Triq Gharb • Map D1 • 2156 1006 • Advance booking essential; closed winter • €€*

6 Ta' Rikardu, Rabat/Victoria, Gozo

A great place for a simple meal of Gozitan cheese, tomatoes and fresh bread, washed down with a sturdy local wine. ✆ *4 Triq Il-Fosos • Map D2 • 2155 5953 • Closes 6pm (7pm in summer) • €*

Rubino, Valletta

For more restaurant listings See pp67, 75, 83, 89, 97 and 103

7 Gesther, Xagħra, Gozo
This simple, old-fashioned country restaurant is a great place to try authentic Maltese dishes at bargain prices. It's very handy for the nearby Ġgantija temples. ◈ *Triq Tmienja Ta' Settembru • Map E1 • 2155 6621 • Closed D, Sun • €*

Grabiel, Marsaskala

8 Grabiel, Marsaskala
Grabiel is justly famous for its fresh and varied seafood. It also serves meat and pasta, but seafood is the star. ◈ *Pjazza Mifsud Bonnici • Map F5 • 2163 4194 • Closed Sun D, Mon L • €€€€*

9 Bacchus, Mdina
This magnificent stone palace boasts a vaulted dining room, exquisite perfumed gardens and a panoramic terrace on the ramparts; few restaurants can compare for sheer romance. Choose from the snack menu during the day or go à la carte in the evening. ◈ *1 Triq Inguanez • Map C4 • 2145 4981 • €€ (snack menu), €€€€€ (à la carte)*

10 Zeri's, Paċeville
Stylish and relaxed, this fashionable place is a wonderfully grown-up oasis amid the frenzy of Paċeville. The chef prepares fresh, creative dishes inspired from around the world. ◈ *19 Triq Paċeville • Map D3 • 2135 9559 • Closed Mon L & D, Tue–Sun L • €€€*

Top 10 Food Shops

1 Smart Supermarket, Birkirkara
A good source of local meat, fresh fish, vegetables and Gozitan cheese. ◈ *Triq In-Naxxar*

2 Azzopardi's Fisheries, Sliema
This shop is highly praised for the variety and freshness of its seafood. ◈ *Triq Tas-Sliema*

3 Wembley Stores, Valletta
A handy convenience store, selling Maltese bread, local cheese, honey and regional wines. ◈ *Triq Ir-Repubblika*

4 Valletta Bus Station
This unlikely venue has stalls selling some of the freshest bread and cakes, and *mqaret* (date pastries).

5 Ir-Razzett, Mellieħa
Delicious fresh fruit and vegetables are the main attraction here. ◈ *244 Triq Ġorġ Borg Olivier*

6 Parruċċan, Rabat
Parruċċan sells traditional cakes and pastries made to generations-old family recipes. ◈ *3 Triq San Cataldus*

7 Fish Market, Marsaxlokk
The busiest and most colourful fish market on the islands, held every Sunday.

8 Marsovin, Marsa
One of Malta's oldest wine-makers; cellar tours (book ahead). ◈ *www.marsovin.com*

9 4 Triq Il Fosos, Rabat /Victoria, Gozo
This shop, next to Ta' Rikardu restaurant, sells traditional Gozitan thyme honey, anisette and local wines.

10 Delicata, Paola
Another leading wine-producer, also offering tours. ◈ *Paola waterfront • 2182 5199*

For a guide to restaurant price ranges See p67

AROUND
MALTA

MALTA'S TOP 10

Left **Grand Master's Palace** Right **Summer dining room, Casa Rocca Piccola**

Around Valletta

VALLETTA, A GLORIOUS CITY OF GOLDEN STONE, *straddles a narrow promontory flanked on either side by magnificent natural harbours. Built for the Knights after the Great Siege of 1565 and named after their victorious Grand Master, Jean Parisot de la Vallette, this fortress city is contained behind a massive ring of impenetrable walls and bastions. Within the walls, the Renaissance streets unfold in an elegant grid. Valletta's heart is broad Triq Ir-Repubblika, Republic Street, lined with princely palaces and dominated by the spectacular Co-Cathedral of St John. From here, side streets flanked by*

crumbling palazzi slope steeply down to the harbours. Time, neglect and the terrible bombardment of World War II have all taken their toll on this miniature capital, and yet its cobbled streets remain hauntingly redolent of the era of the Knights. Still dreaming of the past, the somnolent city shuts down at nightfall.

Manoel Theatre

🔟 Sights

1. St John's Co-Cathedral
2. Palace of the Grand Masters
3. Auberges of the Langues
4. National Museum of Archaeology
5. National Museum of Fine Arts
6. St James Cavalier Centre for Creativity
7. Lascaris War Rooms
8. Manoel Theatre
9. St Paul's Shipwreck Church
10. Casa Rocca Piccola

Preceding pages **A view of Mdina Cathedral from outside the city walls**

St John's Co-Cathedral

St John's Co-Cathedral

Although the magnificent Co-Cathedral may be severe and unembellished on the outside, inside it explodes in a glorious visual paean to the wealth and influence of the powerful Knights *(see pp10–13)*.

Palace of the Grand Masters

This spectacular palace, filled with opulent tapestries and paintings, was the magnificent residence of the Grand Masters of the Order of the Knights of St John for more than two centuries *(see pp8–9)*.

Auberges of the Langues

Each of the eight *langues* – literally "tongues", national branches of the Order of St John – had its own inn, or auberge, in newly built 16th-century Valletta. They were grand lodging houses for the Knights, and monuments to their wealth and prestige. Most of the few surviving auberges are now government offices and are not open to the public, but their graceful Baroque façades epitomize Valletta's regal allure. The most lavish is the Auberge de Castille et Leon (on Misrah Kastilja), now the office of the Maltese president. The former Auberge de Provence houses the National Museum of Archaeology. Look out too for the Auberge d'Italie, on Triq Il-Merkanti, and the discreet Auberge d'Aragon, opposite St Paul's Anglican Cathedral. ◈ *Map H3, H2, H3, J1*

National Museum of Archaeology

The old Auberge de Provence, its former magnificence somewhat battered, is the setting for this collection of fascinating artifacts gathered from Malta's prehistoric temples. Two of the star attractions are the serene and lovely "Sleeping Lady" *(see p40)* and the "Venus of Malta" *(see p14)*.

"Venus of Malta", National Museum of Archaeology

National Museum of Fine Arts

A sweet but rather faded 16th-century *palazzo* with a fine Baroque staircase houses this delightful museum, which contains many paintings, sculptures and items of furniture by Maltese and overseas artists *(see p40)*.

Auberge de Castille et Leon

For more on artifacts discovered in Malta's prehistoric temples See p35

St James Cavalier Centre for Creativity

St James Cavalier Centre for Creativity
One of the mighty bastions that protect the main gate into the city has been sympathetically and beautifully restored. It now houses this excellent centre for contemporary arts, with a theatre, cinema and galleries *(see p40)*. There's also a delightful café, Inspirations, with an outdoor terrace in summer *(see p66)*.

Lascaris War Rooms
These dank, sunless rooms deep in Valletta's bastions were the nerve centre for military operations during World War II. Field Marshal Montgomery and General Eisenhower were among the Allied commanders based here. The wartime atmosphere is recreated with models and equipment, and an audio guide is available *(see p40)*.

Malta and the Movies
Valletta's Grand Harbour is spectacularly cinematic, ringed by honey-coloured spires and bastions which have barely changed in centuries. The Maltese islands have provided the backdrop for countless films, including *Troy, Gladiator, Midnight Express, The League of Extraordinary Gentlemen, Swept Away* and *A Different Loyalty*.

Manoel Theatre
The Manoel is one of the oldest surviving enclosed theatres in Europe. It was built in 1731 by Grand Master Manoel de Vilhena. The auditorium is much smaller than in modern theatres, oval and lined with three tiers of boxes on which a delicate, gilded Mediterranean scene was painted. A particularly lavish box, reserved for the Grand Master, is now used by the Maltese President. A seat is still reserved for the censor, who retains enormous influence in this deeply Catholic country. The stage and orchestra pit are tiny, so large modern productions, such as ballets, can rarely be mounted. The adjoining theatre museum contains fascinating 19th-century machinery for making dramatic sound effects, including thunder and heavy winds. The pretty café is one of the nicest in Valletta *(see p66)*. ✆ Triq It-Teatru L'Antik • Map J2 • 2122 4515 • Guided visits 10:30am, 11:30am and 2:30pm Mon –Fri (including adm to theatre museum) • Adm charge • www.manoeltheatre.org

St Paul's Shipwreck Church
Dedicated to Malta's premier patron saint, this elaborate Baroque church was built between 1639 and 1740 on the site of an earlier, simpler church by Gerolamo Cassar *(see p41)*. The façade was added in 1885 by Nicola Zammit *(see p38)*.

Casa Rocca Piccola
This exquisite palace was built in the 16th century for an Italian Knight, but it has belonged to the noble de Piro family for the last two centuries. The 9th

Marquis de Piro has opened his family home to the public, and runs entertaining and witty guided tours around the 50-room palazzo. (The Marquis doesn't personally lead all the tours, so it's best to ensure in advance that he'll be your guide.) The rooms contain some beautiful items of furniture and fascinating curiosities, such as a pouch of silver medical instruments – among the very few silver objects to survive Napoleon's rapacious troops. There's also an ornate 18th-century sedan chair. The family portraits and photographs, and the quirky curio collections, lend the house a warm and personal ambience not usually found in stately homes. Underneath the palazzo, the old water cisterns were converted into a bomb shelter during World War II. They are connected by passages to the pretty patio with its pots of colourful flowers. ✆ 74 Triq Ir-Repubblika • Map J2 • 2123 1796 • Adm by guided visit only, on the hour 10am–4pm Mon–Sat • Adm charge • www.casaroccapiccola.com

St Paul's Shipwreck Church

A Day in Valletta

Morning

Few city tours begin with bus stations, but Malta's venerable fleet of **antique buses** is a delight. Stop at the *mqaret* stall for a date pastry before heading through the main gate. Sweep down Triq Ir-Repubblika to **St John's Co-Cathedral** (see pp10 –13), the most splendid church in the Maltese islands. After visiting the cathedral, have a coffee out on the square at the **Caffe Cordina** (see p66). Continue down Triq Ir-Repubblika to the charming **Casa Rocca Piccola**, where the Marquis will give you a tour of his family home if you pre-book. Have lunch in the stone courtyard of the lovely **Manoel Theatre** (see p66). Lunchtime concerts are often held here – check in advance with the tourist office.

Afternoon

Return to Triq Ir-Repubblika and make for the Auberge de Provence, now home to the fascinating **National Museum of Archaeology** (see p40). A visit will help you to put Malta's extraordinary temple culture into context. Don't miss the upstairs salon or the beautiful and mysterious megalithic sculpture of the "Sleeping" Lady. Stroll over to the **Upper Barrakka Gardens**, which are small but beautifully kept, for spellbinding views over the Grand Harbour. The view is best at dusk, extending across the water to the romantic silhouette of the Three Cities (see pp68–71). Watch the sun set over a glass of local wine and a light supper at the Café Deux Baronnes (see p66).

Left **Triq Ir-Repubblika** Right **Sapienza's Bookshop**

Shopping

1 "Monti" Market
Crowds pack this street market every morning to buy fashion items, CDs, leather goods, souvenirs and more. There's a bigger market on Sundays in St James's Ditch.
◎ *Triq Il-Merkanti• Map J2*

2 Triq Ir-Repubblika/ Republic Street
Valletta's showcase avenue and the surrounding streets have its biggest concentration of shops. You'll find familiar British high street names alongside souvenir and jewellery shops. ◎ *Map H3–J2*

3 Sapienza's Bookshop
This friendly shop is probably Malta's best for English-language books. Its stock ranges from Malta-related titles (covering everything from temples to cooking) to beach reading.
◎ *26 Triq Ir-Repubblika • Map H2*

4 Diesel
Two Diesel branches are among the several fashion label shops along Merchant Street (others include Dockers, Kookai and Morgan). They offer slick Italian streetwear for men and women. ◎ *Triq Il-Merkanti • Map J2*

5 Marks & Spencer
This outpost of the famed British store has fashion for men, women and children, a small food section (with a selection of international wines), and an airy café. ◎ *44 Triq It-Teatru L'Antik • Map J2*

6 J. Piccinino
Malta's largest women's swimwear retailer offers styles from tiny bikinis to classic black one-pieces. There are many branches across Malta, several of them in Valletta. ◎ *238–9 Triq Ir-Repubblika • Map J2*

7 The Millroom
This small, stylish boutique has a range of unusual designs for women, mostly in linen, silk and other gorgeous fabrics, plus a good range of accessories. Chill-out music and striking African sculptures set the tone.
◎ *307 Triq San Pawl • Map J2*

8 C. Camilleri
This old-fashioned bakery has been selling scrumptious cakes, sweets and confectionery since 1843. Try the local almond pastries, or deliciously sticky doughnuts and iced buns.
◎ *49–51 Triq Il-Merkanti • Map J2*

9 Malta Crafts Centre
This is a good place to find such Maltese specialities as brightly coloured Mdina glass, delicate lace, and handmade woollen jumpers from Gozo.
◎ *Misrah San Ġwann • Map H2*

10 Heritage Malta Giftshop
This large, well-stocked shop at the entrance to the Museum of Archaeology sells its own comprehensive range of books, plus souvenirs and postcards.
◎ *Triq Ir-Repubblika • Map H2*

Right **Tra Buxu** Right **The Pub**

10 Nightlife

1 Maestro e Fresco
Valletta has few late-night bars or clubs, but this relaxed wine bar is a mellow spot for a drink and a snack. At weekends, there are regular live gigs featuring jazz or world music. ◈ *8–9 Triq Nofs In-Nhar • Map H2*

2 The Pub
This tiny hole-in-the-wall pub has a ghoulish claim to fame: it is here that Oliver Reed is said to have drunk himself to death during the filming of the movie *Gladiator*. Photos of the actor adorn the walls. ◈ *136 Triq L'Arcisoof • Map J2*

3 Tra Buxu
Black-and-white photos of musical instruments cover the brick walls of this subterranean wine bar. Laid-back and stylish, it's a great spot to unwind after a hard day's sightseeing. ◈ *1 Triq Id-Dejqa • Map G4*

4 Castille Wine Vaults
This elegant, vaulted wine bar opposite the Castille Hotel offers a good range of local and international wines plus tasty snacks. On some weekends, especially in winter, it hosts live jazz. ◈ *Pjazza Kastilja • Map H3*

5 Sacha's Bar & Bistro
George Curmi, a well-known local musician, owns this buzzy spot, which has live music every night. Check the website for who's on. ◈ *37 Triq Nofs In-Nhar • Map H2 • www.sachasbistro.com*

6 QEII
A friendly and unpretentious little pub, the QEII has a tiny terrace offering great views of the Grand Harbour. Perfect for an early evening drink as the sun sets. ◈ *Triq Il-Mediterran (at entrance to Lower Barrakka Gardens) • Map K2*

7 Labyrinth 1586
Symbolizing the regeneration of once-sleazy Strait Street, Labyrinth 1586 is a stylish fusion of bar, supper club, art gallery and live-music venue. ◈ *44 Triq Id-Dejqa • Map G4*

8 St James Cavalier Centre for Creativity
Valletta's vibrant new arts centre offers a range of activities for the whole family, from cult-film screenings to theatre and dance performances *(see p40)*.

9 Mediterranean Conference Centre
Valletta's handsome conference centre, set in the atmospheric old hospital belonging to the Knights of St John, regularly hosts music, theatre, dance and other events, by local and overseas performers. ◈ *Triq Il-Mediterran • Map K2 • www.mcc.com.mt*

10 Manoel Theatre
This tiny jewel of a theatre makes for an atmospheric night out. Its stage has hosted some major international performers. The courtyard café is perfect for a light lunch *(see p66)*.

Left **Caffe Cordina** Right **Gambrinus**

🔟 Cafés

Caffe Cordina
Valletta's most famous café, the elegant Cordina has a large, shady terrace on the square. The drinks and snacks (which include excellent *pastizzi*) are overpriced, but the location can't be beaten. ◈ *Misrah Ir-Repubblika • Map J2*

Inspirations
Part of the St James Cavalier Centre for Creativity *(see p40)*, Inspirations offers tasty Maltese and Italian dishes plus lighter fare such as soups and quiches. There's a pretty terrace. ◈ *Triq Papa Piju V • Map H3*

Café Jubilee
Small and wood-panelled, with tiny booths, this cosy spot is decorated with old posters. It is a favourite with locals working or shopping nearby, serving good sandwiches and light meals. ◈ *125 Triq Santa Lucija • Map J2*

Deli Café
This simple café offers tasty pasta dishes and sandwiches at bargain prices. Popular with young locals, it's good for a quick stop while sightseeing. ◈ *Messina Palace, 141 Triq San Kristofru • Map J2*

Museum Café
Cluttered and cosy, with old prints and curios in the walls, this is a popular place for breakfast or a mid-morning snack. Try a creamy cappuccino and a couple of ricotta-filled *pastizzi*. ◈ *24 Triq Melita • Map H3*

Café Marquee
One of several cafés on an attractive central square, the shady terrace here has fine views of the cathedral's façade. It serves all the usual favourites – pizzas, pasta, burgers etc. ◈ *9 Misrah San Ġwann • Map H2*

Café Deux Baronnes
An outdoor café with wrought-iron chairs and tables under crisp white parasols, the Café Deux Baronnes offers spectacular views over the whole of the Grand Harbour. ◈ *Upper Barrakka Gardens (lower level), Triq Sant' Orsla • Map H3*

Café Cadena
Popular with business people and elegant ladies taking a break from shopping, this is usually packed at lunchtimes. It serves snacks, drinks and simple meals. ◈ *37-38 Triq Il-Merkanti • Map J2*

Gambrinus Café
Firmly stuck in a 1960s time-warp, this little café has chrome-panelled walls and lipstick-red chairs and tables. The coffee is probably the best in town. ◈ *Triq Melita (corner of Triq Zakkarija) • Map H3*

Café Manoel
This arty, fashionable café is tucked in the Manoel Theatre's courtyard. It serves sandwiches, home-made soups and classic local dishes such as rabbit stew. Opera plays in the background. ◈ *115 Triq It-Teatru L'Antik • Map J2*

Restaurants get busy at lunchtime so you may have to reserve a table then. In the evenings, you'll only have to book at weekends.

Price Categories

For a three course meal for one with half a bottle of wine (or equivalent meal), taxes and extra charges.

€ under 5 Lm/€12
€€ 5–10 Lm/€12–24
€€€ 10–15 Lm/€24–36
€€€€ 15–20 Lm/€36–48
€€€€€ over 20 Lm/€48

Rubino

🔟 Restaurants

1 Malata
Politicians and business people love this smart yet informal restaurant, which offers highly creative, beautifully prepared French fare. It's abuzz with deals at lunchtimes, but evenings are quieter. ❧ *Misrah Il-Palazz • Map J2 • 2123 3967 • Closed Sun • €€€€*

2 Da Pippo
A simple, friendly little trattoria, serving delicious and beautifully fresh local cuisine. There are no printed menus, as the chef uses whatever is freshest at the market that day. Open lunchtimes only *(see p56)*.

3 Giannini Ristorante
One of the finest restaurants in the capital, Giannini's offers sublime views to go with its sophisticated versions of local cuisine *(see p56)*.

4 Rubino Ristorante & Dolceria
A former confectioner's, Rubino's is a great place to try traditional local cooking. Desserts are still the highlight *(see p56)*.

5 Ambrosia
This coolly elegant wine bar tucked down a side street serves creative and beautifully fresh Mediterranean cuisine in a welcoming and informal atmosphere. Save room for the heavenly desserts. ❧ *137 Triq L'Arcisoof • Map J2 • 2122 5923 • Closed Mon D, Sun L & D • €€*

6 The Carriage
This elegant hideaway offers sophisticated Mediterranean cuisine on a romantic terrace in summer, or in a chic dining room in winter. ❧ *22/5 Valletta Buildings, Triq Nofs In-Nhar • Map H2 • 2124 7828 • Closed Mon–Thu D, Sun • €€€€€*

7 Blue Room
When pasta and pizza pall, try the comfortable and elegant Blue Room – consistently voted Valletta's favourite Chinese restaurant. ❧ *59 Triq Ir-Repubblika • Map J2 • 2123 8014 • €€€*

8 Crianza
This cheap and cheerful little pizza joint is in a cosy vaulted cellar. It serves pasta and salads as well as imaginatively-topped pizzas. ❧ *33 Triq L'Arcisoof • Map J2 • 2123 8120 • Closed Sun L • €*

9 Sicilia
The dining room is tiny, but a terrace offers picture-postcard views over the Grand Harbour. Try the tasty pasta dishes or the fresh fish. Open lunchtimes only. ❧ *1A Triq San Ġwann (above Victoria Gate) • Map J3 • 2124 0569 • Closed Mon–Sat D, Sun • €€*

10 Trattoria Palazz
This attractive, stone-walled subterranean restaurant is cool in summer but cosy in winter. The grilled meats and seafood are good, but the pasta is better. ❧ *43 Triq It-Teatru L'Antik • Map J2 • 2122 6611 • Closed Sat–Sun L • €€€*

Left **Armstrong 100-ton gun, Fort Rinella** Right **Spinola Bay, St Julian's**

Around Sliema, St Julian's and the Three Cities

VALLETTA'S CLOSE NEIGHBOURS – *Sliema and St Julian's to the west, the Three Cities (Vittoriosa, Senglea and Kalkara) to the east – couldn't be more different. The Three Cities, piled on a pair of promontories jutting into the bay, are quiet, historic and time-worn, a far cry from the brash glitz of Sliema and St Julian's, where high-rise hotels, luxury apartments, shopping centres and neon-lit nightclubs have mushroomed, popular with tourists and young locals alike.*

TOP 10 Sights

1. The Inquisitor's Palace, Vittoriosa
2. Collachio, Vittoriosa
3. Church of St Lawrence, Vittoriosa
4. Our Lady of Victories Church, Senglea
5. Fort Rinella, Kalkara
6. Paceville
7. Fort St Angelo, Vittoriosa
8. Malta Maritime Museum, Vittoriosa
9. Triq It-Torri, Sliema
10. Spinola Bay, St Julian's

Gardens of the Inquisitor's Palace

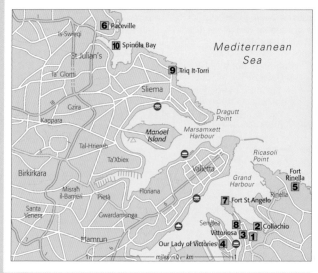

1 The Inquisitor's Palace, Vittoriosa

In the late 1500s, word of the lax and frivolous lifestyle of the Knights in Malta reached the ears of the Pope in Rome. An Inquisitor was dispatched to the islands, with orders to bring the Knights to heel. This palace was not simply the Inquisitor's residence; it also served as court and prison. But today there is little sense of its former magnificence, or even of its former role. Only some 17th-century murals, a few cells, and the grand staircase survive. The Judgement Room strikes the only chilling note: prisoners entered the Inquisitor's presence through a half-sized door, forcing even the most defiant to bow. ◈ *Triq Il-Mina L-Kbira • Map L5 • 2182 7006 • 9am–5pm daily • Adm charge • www.heritagemalta.org*

2 Collachio, Vittoriosa

Collachio is the area of Vittoriosa where the Knights built their auberges (inns) when they first arrived in Malta in the 1530s. This cool stone maze remains the most atmospheric district in the Three Cities, a place to abandon the map and lose yourself in the

Collachio

Our Lady of Victories Church, Senglea

drowsy lanes. None of the auberges are currently open to the public, although the Auberge de France – now the Museum of the Maltese Language – may take visitors by prior arrangement. Very little has survived from the time of the Normans in Malta, but look out for an exquisitely carved Siculo-Norman window in the crumbling but picturesque old mansion at 11 Triq It-Tramuntana. ◈ *Map L5*

3 Church of St Lawrence, Vittoriosa

A church has stood on this site for 900 years. The present elegant Baroque church was built by Lorenzo Gafa in 1681, and, after substantial bomb damage during World War II, has been lovingly restored *(see p38)*.

4 Our Lady of Victories Church, Senglea

This church remains close to the hearts of the Maltese, thanks to two much-venerated statues: the jewel-encrusted 17th-century statue of our Blessed Lady of Victories, and a statue of Christ the Redeemer which is widely believed to have miraculous healing powers *(see p38)*.

The Lookout

Out at the very tip of Senglea, the gardens of Ġnien Il-Gardjola contain a small but much-photographed *vedette* (lookout). Jutting out over the heights of Senglea Point, it frames a beautiful view of the Grand Harbour. The *vedette* is famously carved with symbols of vigilance: an eye, an ear and a crane. These were supposed to remind the sentries of their duty of watchfulness. The *vedette* was carefully dismantled and stored before World War II, and thus survived the bombs.

Fort Rinella, Kalkara

Rinella was one of a pair of coastal batteries built in the 1880s by the British, against threats from Italy. It was equipped with a huge Armstrong 100-ton gun, but the introduction of quick-firing guns only 20 years later rendered this mighty weapon obsolete. A group of enthusiastic young men in Victorian garb stage an "animated tour" – letting off cannons, firing muskets and signalling furiously – to provide an enjoyable insight into the fort's history. (The 100-ton gun itself has only been fired once in recent years, causing the fort's ceilings to crack, so it now remains silent.) ◈ *Triq Santu Rokku • Map E4 • 10am–5pm daily; animated tour 2:30pm daily • Adm charge • www.wirtartna.org/FortRinella/fortrinella.htm*

Paċeville

Paċeville comprises a handful of small streets and alleys packed with bars, clubs and restaurants. On Saturday nights, the area is thronged with party people, both Maltese and tourists, all dressed to kill. Your feelings about Paċeville will probably depend on your age and notions of what constitutes a good holiday. All those under 25 in search of booze, bright lights and bars will find Paċeville the answer to every hedonistic dream. Everyone else will feel more comfortable in nearby St Julian's and Spinola Bay, where the restaurants and bars are geared towards an older and calmer clientele. ◈ *Map P1*

Fort St Angelo, Vittoriosa

This mighty fortress dominates the theatrical sweep of the Grand Harbour. Perhaps nothing evokes the drama of the Great Siege of 1565 like its imposing bulk when viewed from across the water in Valletta. Seat of the Grand Master until Valletta, the Knights' new capital, was constructed, it was here that punishment was meted out. Most feared was the "oubliette" – a pit hollowed out of the rock where wrong-doers were abandoned to the darkness and their own demons. The fortress withstood the Turks in 1565 and the German bombs in the 1940s, and these two great sieges are discussed in the fascinating guided tours that take place every day. ◈ *Map K4 • 10am–5pm daily • Adm charge*

Paċeville nightlife

ort St Angelo

8 Malta Maritime Museum, Vittoriosa

The grand 19th-century building overlooking Vittoriosa's seafront was built by the British to house the naval bakery. Now it contains a museum celebrating Malta's seafaring tradition *(see p41)*.

9 Triq It-Torri, Sliema

Sliema, once a small fishing village and modest resort, is now a dense concrete jungle packed with hotels, shops, restaurants and bars. But some old-fashioned traditions have survived – notably the *passeggiata*, the traditional evening stroll imported from Italy. Each evening, couples and families amble along Sliema's seafront, Triq It-Torri (Tower Rd), nodding to neighbours and sizing up strangers. Pavement cafés make people-watching easier. The stretch from Ghar Id-Dud to St Julian's Point is the most popular. ◈ *Map Q2*

10 Spinola Bay, St Julian's

There is little natural beauty in the concrete sprawl of Malta's northern coast, but Spinola Bay, with its smattering of pretty villas, is a welcome exception. The small bay has become one of the most fashionable addresses in Malta. A clutch of smart restaurants with terraces overlook the bay. Multicoloured *luzzus* sway gently in the sun, as fishermen by the water's edge mend their nets. The bay is prettiest at night, when the twinkling lights are reflected in the water. ◈ *Map P1*

A Walk around the Three Cities

Morning

🕐 Before you start out, note that there are very few places for lunch or coffee in the **Three Cities**, so make sure to bring snacks and water. Enter **Vittoriosa** through its mighty main gate (where there is a very nice outdoor café for a coffee break) and head along Triq Il-Mina l-Kbira. On the right, you'll come to the **Inquisitor's Palace**, where unfortunate prisoners were accused of heresy. Behind the Inquisitor's Palace is the original Knights' quarter, called the **Collachio**. Head down Triq H. Tabone to see the **auberges** (inns) of the Knights, before returning to the central square, Misrah Ir Rebh. There are a couple of simple bars here if you want to stop for a snack or a coffee.

Afternoon

Wind your way down to the water's edge at Dockyard Creek. The **Freedom Monument**, in front of the splendid **Church of St Lawrence** commemorates those who died during World War II. Take a boat tour around the **Grand Harbour** (there are regular departures from the waterfront in Vittoriosa) for sublime views of Valletta and the Three Cities. Continue your stroll around the bay, following the water's edge to the entrance to **Senglea**. Walk down Senglea's main street, Triq Il-Vitorja, to the gardens right at the tip of the promontory; here you will find the famous **vedette** (**lookout**) with its curious symbols, offering more magnificent views.

St Julian's was originally known as San Giljan; its name was anglicized by British soldiers in the 19th century.

Left **Eighteen-Ninety** Right **Victor's Jewellery**

Shopping

Bay Street Mall, St Julian's
The biggest mall in Malta has branches of all the major chains (including most British and Italian high-street names), plus cafés, restaurants and kids' play areas. ◈ *St George's Bay • Map D3*

Plaza Shopping Mall, Sliema
Sliema's main shopping mall has high-street chains like Body Shop and Benetton, along with cafés and a well-stocked book-shop, Agenda. ◈ *Triq Bisazza • Map R3*

Chaucer's, St Julian's
This convenient newsagent's sells a wide range of books and magazines in several languages. There's plenty of choice if you are looking for relaxing beach reading. ◈ *Bay Street Tourist Complex, Level 1, St George's Bay • Map D3*

Eighteen-Ninety, Sliema
Elegant and stylish furnishings and decorative objects for the home are sold here, along with table linen, women's fashion, fine wines and gourmet foods. It's a good place to find unusual gifts. ◈ *Annunciation Square • Map R3*

Cesca's, Sliema
One of a popular chain of shoe stores, Cesca's sells a wide variety of footwear for men and women, especially Italian labels. It also carries a range of accessories. ◈ *Triq Bisazza • Map R3*

Go Bananas, St Julian's
This is a convenient place to pick up local Maltese specialities including Mdina glass, lace, honey, woollen jumpers and the famous Maltese Cross in gold or silver. ◈ *107 Triq San Ġorġ • Map P1*

Bisazza Street, Sliema
As well as the Plaza Shopping Centre *(see left)* and a supermarket, all the usual high street chains can be found on or around Sliema's Bisazza Street, including Next, Mango and dozens more. ◈ *Map R3*

Pedigree Toyshops, St Julian's
This branch of one of Malta's biggest toy retailers has all you need to keep young kids happy indoors, on the beach, or on the plane. It's also a good back-up on a rainy day ◈ *Bay Street Tourist Complex, Level 0, St George's Bay • Map D3*

Victor's Jewellery, Sliema
Malta has long been known for its delicate filigree jewellery. This store has a good range of locally made examples as well as Maltese Crosses in gold or silver ◈ *7 Triq It-Torri • Map R3*

Tower Stores, Sliema
Village shops and fruit-and-vegetable vans supply most visitors' needs, but occasionally a supermarket comes in useful. There are few in Malta; this is the biggest in the Sliema region. ◈ *Triq Ir-Kbira • Map R3*

Left **BJ's Nightclub and Piano Bar** Right **Dragonara Palace Casino**

⁷⁰/₁₀ Nightlife

1 The Alley, Paċeville
A long-standing favourite in Paċeville, with a happy young crowd and DJs at weekends. During the week, there are occasional live gigs – check the website. ✪ *Triq Wilġa• Map P1 • www.at-the-alley.com*

2 BJs Nightclub and Piano Bar, Paċeville
A classic in Paċeville, BJs has great live bands playing everything from jazz to rock at weekends. It's quieter during the week, when a 30-something crowd enjoy chilling out on the battered sofas. ✪ *Triq Ball • Map P1*

3 Coconut Grove, Paċeville
Brash and noisy, this is a huge hit with local teenagers (it's strictly for the under-20s). To fit in, dress to impress – boys as well as girls. ✪ *Triq Wilġa • Map P1*

4 Fuego, St Julian's
With its tropical cocktails, over-the-top Caribbean decor, and DJs playing Latin rhythms, Fuego may be a tad tacky, but it's always good for a fun night out. There are free salsa lessons on Thursdays. ✪ *Triq Santu Wistin, St George's Bay • Map D3*

5 Clique, Paċeville
This hugely popular dance club brings in top international DJs to supplement the great local line-up. House music for a young and up-for-it crowd. ✪ *83 Triq San Ġorġ • Map P1*

6 Misfits Bar, Paċeville
A dimly lit, boho-chic spot, Misfits makes a change from the hormone-fuelled atmosphere elsewhere in Paċeville. Chill-out gives way to dance music at weekends. ✪ *Triq Paċeville • Map P1*

7 121, St Julian's
A sophisticated and sultry lounge bar with sleek designer furnishings and deep sofas to sink into. The early evening lounge music progresses to jazzy house and soul as the night heats up. ✪ *St George's Bay • Map D3*

8 Casino de Venezia, Vittoriosa
Malta's newest casino is in a stunning palace on the Vittoriosa waterfront, offering romantic views of Valletta across the Grand Harbour. Yachties and well-heeled locals try their luck at the tables. ✪ *Palazzo del Capitan • Map K4*

9 Dragonara Palace Casino, St Julian's
This 19th-century palazzo by the sea is Malta's most lavish casino, with gaming tables, slot machines and live entertainment. Dress smartly and take ID – it's for over-18s only. ✪ *Dragonara Point • Map E3*

10 Eden SuperBowl and Cinemas, St Julian's
Malta's biggest cinema complex cum bowling alley has 16 screens showing Hollywood's best, plus an Imax cinema. ✪ *St George's Bay • Map D3*

Take note: nightclubs in Malta change names or close down with alarming frequency.

Left **Café Giorgio** Right **Café Juliani**

Bars and Cafés

Café Juliani, St Julian's
Part of the chic Hotel Juliani *(see p113)*, this fashionable café is perfect for a delicious lunch, afternoon tea, or just a cocktail. Sunday brunch, complete with a stack of international newspapers, is an institution. ◈ *12 Triq San Ġorġ • Map P1*

Cara's Café, Sliema
Popular with tourists and local workers alike, this bustling café has a great location on Sliema's seafront promenade. It serves snacks and light meals, but the cakes are the real highlight. ◈ *249 Triq It-Torri • Map Q2*

Café Giorgio, Sliema
The perfect people-watching spot on Sliema's seafront. Soak up the evening sun on the terrace while the Maltese stroll past during their *passeggiata*. ◈ *Triq Ix-Xatt Ta' Tigne • Map R3*

Caesar's Café, Portomaso
A spacious café overlooking the yachts bobbing in the marina. Try the huge breakfast pancakes, or the tasty meals and snacks served all day. A good family spot. ◈ *Portomaso Marina • Map P1*

The Bar, St Julian's
A slick little bar with a stylish mix of contemporary and retro furnishings. Drop by for a glass of wine or a cocktail, and stick around for one of the regular live gigs. ◈ *32 Balluta Buildings, Balluta Bay • Map P2*

Simon's Pub, Sliema
This local favourite is in a residential district a few streets back from the seafront. Less frenetic than the seaside bars, it's still lively and serves great cocktails. ◈ *115 Triq Depiro • Map Q2*

Places, Paceville
Trendy young clubbers meet at this buzzy bar in the heart of Paceville. At weekends, it doubles as a small dance venue with DJs, but it's quieter during the week. ◈ *Triq Ball • Map P1*

Vinotheque Wine & Cheese Bar, St Julian's
A bright and breezy wine bar in a smart hotel offers an excellent array of local and overseas wines accompanied by light meals and snacks. There's a terrace for relaxing in summer. ◈ *Corinthia Marina Hotel, St George's Bay • Map D3*

Plough & Anchor, Sliema
This cosy, nautically-themed English-style pub stands on Sliema's lively seafront. It offers snacks, or you could try the very decent upstairs restaurant. ◈ *263 Triq It-Torri • Map Q2*

Gelateria Lungomare, Sliema
One of the best ice-cream stands in town, the Lungomare has a choice of over 30 flavours. Go for the rich, dark chocolate or try something unusual such as crème caramel. ◈ *Triq It-Torri, next to the New Tower Palace Hotel • Map R2*

Price Categories

For a three course meal for one with half a bottle of wine (or equivalent meal), taxes and extra charges.

€ under 5 Lm/€12
€€ 5–10 Lm/€12–24
€€€ 10–15 Lm/€24–36
€€€€ 15–20 Lm/€36–48
€€€€€ over 20 Lm/€48

Zeri's Restaurant

🔟 Restaurants

1 Zeri's, Paceville
A stylish but relaxed place serving highly creative cuisine at very reasonable prices *(see p57)*.

2 Mezè, St Julian's
Mezè, one of the hottest bars in town, is in the basement of the trendy Hotel Juliani. In summer it makes way for Eau Zone, serving alfresco seafood dinners on the roof terrace. ◈ *12 Triq San Ġorġ • Map P1 • 2137 6444 • Closed summer, Mon & Tue D in winter • €€€*

3 The Avenue, Paceville
Kids love this hugely popular restaurant, which is brightly decorated in bold colours. It serves great pizzas and pasta at bargain prices. Book in advance or be prepared to queue. ◈ *Triq Gort • Map P1 • 2135 1753 • €€*

4 L'Ordine, St Julian's
A traditional restaurant, L'Ordine recalls the era of the Knights with its wrought-iron furniture and suits of armour. Enjoy fine Italian cuisine, and particularly good fresh fish. ◈ *47 Main Street, Balluta Bay • Map P2 • 2138 2923 • Closed Mon–Sat L • €€€*

5 Barracuda, St Julian's
Set in a handsome villa leaning out over the water, this elegant and romantic restaurant is well-known for its superb seafood. Maltese dishes such as rabbit stew are also on the menu. ◈ *194 Main St, Balluta Bay • Map P2 • 2133 1817 • €€€€€*

6 La Maltija, Paceville
Charmingly out-of-place in the raucous frenzy of Paceville, this rustic-style restaurant serves traditional Maltese dishes. ◈ *1 Triq Il-Knisja • Map P1 • 2135 9602 • Closed L daily, Sun D • €€€*

7 The Kitchen, Sliema
This new restaurant with an award-winning chef is fast gaining popularity with locals and visitors alike. Booking advised. ◈ *210 Triq It-Torri • Map R2 • 2131 1112 • €€€*

8 San Giuliano, St Julian's
Fabulous sea views combine with fine Italian cuisine at the elegant San Giuliano. Highlights include spaghetti with sea urchin sauce, and ultra-fresh seafood. ◈ *3 Triq San Gusepp, Spinola Bay • Map P1 • 2135 2000 • Closed Mon L, three weeks in Jan • €€€€*

9 Peppino's, St Julian's
Brick walls, sea views and check tablecloths set the tone of the smart restaurant upstairs, but the cosy wine bar downstairs is better value. Book early for an outdoor table. ◈ *31 Triq San Ġorġ • Map P1 • 2137 3200 • Closed Sun • €€ (wine bar), €€€ (restaurant)*

10 Blue Elephant, St Julian's
This romantic restaurant serves the finest Thai cuisine in Malta. Dine on the terrace overlooking the marina, or enjoy the lavish rainforest decor inside. ◈ *Hilton Hotel, Portomaso • Map P1 • 2138 3383 • Closed L daily • €€€€*

In Jan 2008, Malta abandons the Maltese lira (Lm) and adopts the euro (€); the price categories above refer to both currencies.

Left **Għadira Wetland Reserve** Right **Baħar Iċ-Ċagħaq**

Around Northern Malta

ORTHERN MALTA HAS AN UNUSUALLY DIVERSE RANGE *of attractions. Some of the island's boldest and brashest resorts can be found here – in particular the summer party capital of Buġibba. St Paul's Bay and the resort of Mellieħa are somewhat quieter, appreciated by families and older visitors alike. The golden sands at Mellieħa Bay are the most popular* on the island, but there are plenty of other beaches to choose from. If the kids ever get bored of the sun, sea and sand, Malta's top family attractions are clustered here – from water parks to the Popeye Village film set. Then there's a wilder side of Malta: stunning cliff walks, extra-ordinary coastal scenery and remote coves, especially along the western end of Marfa Ridge. For wild Malta of a different kind, visit the Għadira Wetland Reserve. Last but not least, there's ancient Malta, represented by the Skorba and Ta Ħaġrat Temples.

Mġarr

🔟 Sights

1. Mellieħa
2. Għadira Wetland Reserve
3. St Paul's Bay
4. Buġibba and Qawra
5. Baħar Iċ-Ċagħaq (White Rocks)
6. Marfa Ridge
7. Popeye Village, Anchor Bay
8. Mġarr
9. Ta' Ħaġrat Temple
10. Skorba Temples

Preceding pages **The patterned interior of the Church of Santa Marija Assunta, Mosta – generally known as Mosta Dome** *(see p85)*

St Paul's Bay

dominates the ornithological year, so the birds you see will depend very much on the season. ◈ *Il-Għadira, Mellieħa Bay • Map A2 • 2134 7646 • Buses 44, 45 • Open Dec–Jan: 9:30am–3:30pm Sat–Sun; Feb–May, Nov: 10:30am–4:30pm Sat–Sun. Closed Jun–Oct • Free (but donations accepted) • www.birdlifemalta.org*

Mellieħa
The family resort of Mellieħa sprawls on a ridge overlooking the curve of Mellieħa Bay *(see p46)*. It's a large resort, but remains fairly low-key, except during the mad months of July and August. Although Mellieħa was one of the first parishes in Malta, the original 15th-century settlement proved too hard to defend from pirates and was soon abandoned. Now its *raison d'être* is tourism, and holiday-makers are drawn by the attractive sandy strip in the bay. Look out for the little shrine of Our Lady of Mellieħa. ◈ *Map B2*

Għadira Wetland Reserve
The illegal hunting and trapping of birds in Malta *(see p111)* has long caused international outrage. This wetland reserve, set just behind the sandy beach at Mellieħa, was established as a safe haven for migrating birds by BirdLife, the local chapter of an international conservation group. They have gained considerable support from the people of Malta over the last few years, and a second reserve, near Xemxija, has also opened. Open days and family days are regularly organized, and volunteers give guided tours of the reserve at weekends. In Malta, more than almost anywhere else, migration

St Paul's Bay
The prettiest of the resorts around the bay of the same name, St Paul's Bay retains some vestiges of the salty old fishing cove from which it developed. It has no beaches, but there are some stretches of flat rocks on which to sunbathe *(see p46)*.

Buġibba and Qawra
Big, brash Buġibba and its marginally quieter neighbour Qawra are two of the islands' largest resorts. Both are geared essentially towards the package tourism market; in summer, most of the hotels are block-booked by tour operators. Buġibba has the greatest concentration of night-life, so you might get a better night's sleep in Qawra. Both offer lidos, boat trips and watersports. It can be hard to get around without your own transport, but you can take excursions if you don't want to hire a car. ◈ *Map C3*

Buġibba

Marfa Ridge

5 Baħar Iċ-Ċagħaq (White Rocks)

It's difficult to understand why this small bay remains so popular with local Maltese families, since it's very close to the main road and there's no sandy beach. Since the establishment here of two – for Malta, at least – sizeable family attractions, Mediterraneo Marine Park and the Splash & Fun Park (see p52), it's even more hectic, especially at weekends and in summer. It's served by ice-cream and snack vans in summer, and there are cafés in both of the fun parks. ✆ Map D3

St Paul in Malta

According to legend, Saint Paul was shipwrecked in AD 60 in the bay now known as St Paul's Bay. He was attacked by a poisonous viper but, to the astonishment of the local people, survived completely unhurt. (A waspish Maltese saying suggests that when the venom left Malta's vipers, it entered the tongues of Maltese women.) St Paul went on to convert the Roman governor Publius to Christianity, and appointed him first bishop of Malta. There are numerous sites dedicated to the saint throughout the islands, all the focus of intense devotion and pilgrimage.

6 Marfa Ridge

On a map, the Marfa Ridge looks like a fish's tail tacked onto the round body of the island. The main landmarks are the storybook crenellations of the Red Tower and the towering cliffs of Ras Il-Qammieħ. The coastline is pitted with numerous coves and beaches, and the whole area is a paradise for walkers (see pp43, 45).

7 Popeye Village, Anchor Bay

Anchor Bay was originally named after the scores of stone Roman anchors that washed up there. Since 1980, it has been known for a Hollywood film set – the Popeye Village (see p52).

Popeye Village

8 Mġarr

There are two places called Mġarr in the Maltese islands: the harbour in Gozo where the ferry arrives, and this sleepy little village on the island of Malta. The locals' pride and joy is the "Egg Church", built in the 1930s with funds raised by the sale of eggs. You can also explore an underground shelter used during World War II, where the rooms have been refurbished to look as they would have during the bombardment of Malta in the 1940s. Mġarr is a good place to try the typically Maltese dish of *fenek*, or rabbit, cooked in various ways *(see p54)*. The important Ta' Ħaġrat and Skorba temples *(see below)* are also in the vicinity. ◈ *Map B3*

9 Ta' Ħaġrat Temple

This temple, near Mġarr, was probably linked in ancient times to those at Skorba, about 1km (half a mile) away. It was first excavated in the 1920s by the celebrated Maltese archeologist Sir Themistocles Zammit, who discovered that it had been built over an earlier village. There is little to see, but the rural setting is very attractive *(see p34)*.

10 Skorba Temples

The Skorba Temples at Żebbiegħ, along with those at Ġgantija on Gozo *(see p35)* are believed to be among the oldest freestanding structures in the world. Excavations have unearthed even earlier shrines in the same location. Although the site has provided significant information for archeologists, there is surprisingly little to see. Look out for the libation holes, bored into the paving slabs at the entrance. Many of the temples have this feature; it has been suggested that the blood of sacrificed animals was poured down these holes to propitiate the gods. The site looks its best in early spring, when the surrounding countryside is green and lush *(see p34)*.

Skorba Temples

A Drive around Northern Malta

Morning

This trip starts from and ends at **Mellieħa**. If the nearby **Ghadira Wetland Reserve** is open, take one of the fascinating guided tours around this sanctuary for wetland birds. This is especially recommended during the spring and autumn migratory seasons. Otherwise, head west to **Popeye Village** for an enjoyable tour around the old film set. Have a quick dip in the sea at the tiny beach. Take the main road from Mellieħa up to the **Marfa Ridge**. Stop by the Red Tower to enjoy the views of Gozo and Comino, then continue to **Ras Il-Qammieħ** (Qammieħ Point) to see the spectacular cliffs. Return to Mellieħa on the main road, and continue to **St Paul's Bay**. Have a lazy lunch overlooking the bay at **Gillieru**.

Afternoon

Follow the road for 4 km (2 miles) through the fertile **Pwales Valley**, with its green fields girdled by tumbling stone walls. Park at the top of the cliff and make the descent via almost two hundred stone steps to **Għajn Tuffieħa** beach. Stretch out and work on your tan for a couple of hours. If you are feeling more active, you could hike around the headland to the busier bay at **Golden Beach**, or perhaps take a boat trip to the quiet cove at **Fomm Ir-Riħ**. The little village of **Mġarr** is famous for its old-fashioned Maltese cooking. Try some typical local rabbit (or simply a drink) at the Friend-to-All Bar on the village square.

Around Northern Malta

Left **Għajn Tuffieħa Bay** Right **Fomm Ir-Riħ Bay**

TOP 10 Beaches and Bays

1 Paradise Bay
A snug bay with a crescent of sand reached by a flight of steps cut into the rock. It's a very popular spot, best during the week or out of season. Bring your snorkel. ◎ *Map A2*

2 Ġnejna Bay
This is a picturesque bay with a small stretch of sand in the middle of a wide arc of flat rocks, backed by creamy limestone cliffs. A handful of boathouses overlook tiny coves. It's a favourite with local families. ◎ *Map A3*

3 Għajn Tuffieħa Bay
A beautiful bay set against terraced hills, with wonderful cliff walks stretching off in either direction *(see p46)*.

4 Golden Bay
This sandy beach is easily accessible and offers several amenities including canoe and pedalo rental. The beach is subject to dangerous currents from time to time; don't swim if the red flag is flying. ◎ *Map A3*

5 Mellieħa Beach
It's hard to believe, but this narrow crescent of shoreline is Malta's largest sandy beach. Unfortunately, it's backed by a main road, but this and its location make it easy to reach by bus or car. It's very popular with families, and has excellent amenities *(see p46)*.

6 Little Armier
There are two Armier beaches – Armier and Little Armier. The first is scruffy and rather unappealing, but the latter is a sandy little cove with a basic beach café. ◎ *Map B2*

7 Salina Bay
The broad sweep of Salina Bay is lined with hotels and apartment blocks. Although there is no beach as such, the flat rocks are good for sunbathing, and the shallow waters are perfect for a dip. The bay gets its name from the nearby salt pans. ◎ *Map C3*

8 Mistra Bay
It's easy to miss the turning for this delightful little strand near Xemxija: A country road scented with honeysuckle leads to the narrow bay where the swimming and snorkelling are good and relatively undisturbed. ◎ *Map B2*

9 Fomm Ir-Riħ Bay
This wild and beautiful beach is difficult to get to; as a result few people make it here except in the very height of summer *(see p44)*.

10 Anchor Bay
This pretty little cove next to the touristy Popeye Village *(see p52)* somehow gets overlooked by the crowds. The sandy beach is little larger than a handkerchief, but it's a good spot for a picnic. ◎ *Map A3*

Price Categories

For a three course meal for one with half a bottle of wine (or equivalent meal), taxes and extra charges.

€	under 5 Lm/€12
€€	5–10 Lm/€12–24
€€€	10–15 Lm/€24–36
€€€€	15–20 Lm/€36–48
€€€€€	over 20 Lm/€48

Il-Vecċja Restaurant & Wine Bar

🔟 Restaurants

1 The Arches, Mellieħa
Lovely and light-filled, with a small covered terrace, The Arches serves some of Malta's best French cuisine. The service and wine list are excellent. ◎ *113 Triq Il-Kbira • Map B3 • 2152 3460 • Closed Mon–Sat L, Sun • €€€€€*

2 Gillieru, St Paul's Bay
A large, family-friendly place with a perfect setting overlooking the bay, Gillieru is good for lunch, dinner or just a coffee break. Try the ultra-fresh fish. ◎ *66 Triq Il-Knisja • Map C3 • 2157 3480 • €€€€*

3 Friend-to-All Bar
Three Mġarr bars are known for traditional rabbit dishes. This simple spot is perhaps the friendliest and certainly the cheapest. Rabbit, cooked various ways, is all that's on the menu. ◎ *Mġarr village square • Map B3 • 2157 3235 • Closed Sun, Mon L • €*

4 Porto del Sol, Xemxija
This relaxed hotel-restaurant overlooking St Paul's Bay serves fresh fish, grilled meats, pasta dishes and tasty local vegetables. ◎ *13 Telghet Ix-Xemxija, St Paul's Bay • Map B3 • 2157 3970 • Closed Sun in summer, D daily in winter • €€€*

5 Giuseppi's Restaurant & Wine Bar, Mellieħa
Traditional dishes are given a contemporary twist. Locals rave about rabbit with bitter chocolate sauce. ◎ *25 Triq Sant' Elena • Map B3 • 2158 6401 • Closed L, Sun, Mon • €€€€*

6 Savini, Qawra
This beautifully converted farmhouse is now a charming restaurant. Dine on lobster or venison on a lovely terrace overlooking the countryside. ◎ *Triq Il-Qawra • Map C3 • 2157 6927 • Closed L daily • €€€€€*

7 Ciao Bella Pizzeria, St Paul's Bay
A reliable, family-friendly place serving tasty pasta, pizza, meat and fish dishes at bargain prices. The portions are large and the service fast. ◎ *Triq Il-Mosta • Map C3 • 2158 0112 • Closed L daily • €*

8 Il-Vecċja Restaurant & Wine Bar, St Paul's Bay
A characterful 18th-century inn perched beside the picturesque harbour. Menu highlights include fresh fish and Maltese rabbit stew. ◎ *372 Triq San Pawl • Map C3 • 2158 2376 • Closed Mon–Sat L • €€*

9 Xatba, Mellieħa
Rich pasta and risotto dishes, perfectly prepared fresh fish and grilled meats are served at this family-run restaurant, a favourite with locals and tourists. ◎ *Triq Il-Marfa • Map B3 • 2152 1753 • Closed L daily • €€*

10 Wild Thyme, St Paul's Bay
This pretty, rustic restaurant serves tender veal and chicken, home-made pasta and wonderful fresh seafood. Veggies are well catered for. ◎ *Triq L'Imgiebah, Xemxija Heights • Map C3 • 2157 2202 • €€€*

Left **Mdina** Right **"Clapham Junction" Cart Ruts**

Around Central Malta

POISED ON A PLATEAU IN THE VERY CENTRE OF THE ISLAND, *Mdina* is Malta's ancient capital and its most beautiful city. Its streets are charged with history, and, particularly after dusk, each faded palace and medieval chapel seems to whisper its secrets. Nearby Rabat is just as old and has a special place in the hearts of the devout Maltese: it was here that St Paul was supposedly brought after the shipwreck in AD 60. To the south, the gorgeous Dingli Cliffs are perfect for hiking and picnicking, with fine views, while the shady Buskett Gardens offer respite from the summer heat, and the Bronze-Age cart ruts of "Clapham Junction" remain mysterious. Mosta is dominated – as is much of the island – by the enormous dome of its parish church, which miraculously escaped destruction during World War II.

Verdala Palace and Buskett Gardens

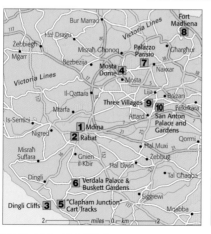

🔟 Sights

1. **Mdina**
2. **Rabat**
3. **Dingli Cliffs**
4. **Mosta Dome, Mosta**
5. **"Clapham Junction" Cart Ruts, Msierah**
6. **Verdala Palace and Buskett Gardens**
7. **Palazzo Parisio, Naxxar**
8. **Fort Madliena, Madliena**
9. **The Three Villages (Balzan, Lija and Attard)**
10. **San Anton Palace Gardens, Attard**

Mdina

1 Mdina dreams quietly behind her impenetrable walls. Time stopped for the ancient Maltese capital when the seafaring Knights arrived in the 1530s, settling around the Grand Harbour – and sidelining Mdina and its inhabitants in the process. "The Silent City", as it is still known, may fill up with tourists by day, but the hush returns with nightfall when the crowds depart. If you can, explore this lovely city by day, and again by night *(see pp16–17)*.

Rabat

2 Rabat and Mdina were once a single entity, before the Arabs walled and fortified Mdina almost a thousand years ago. Rabat retains the islands' most evocative Roman remains in its Domus Romanus. The remnants of this once opulent Roman villa are beside a small museum containing fine mosaics and frescoes from the Roman era. Many of

Rabat – St Agatha and St Paul

Malta's most deeply resonant religious sites are concentrated in Rabat. They include the grotto where St Paul is said to have lived after he was shipwrecked, extensive catacombs dating back to the very early years of Christianity and a cave painted with 14th-century murals where St Agatha is said to have hidden *(see pp16–17)*.

Mosta Dome

Dingli Cliffs

Dingli Cliffs

3 The spectacular Dingli Cliffs are wild and undeveloped – a rare treat on the crowded little island of Malta. They provide the perfect terrain for walking and picnics, with fine views out to little Filfla Island *(see p43)*.

Mosta Dome, Mosta

4 It's impossible to miss the gigantic dome of Mosta's parish church, which is visible from much of the island. Once the third-largest dome in Europe, it was relegated to fourth place in 1971 when the Xewkija Rotunda in Gozo was completed – at least according to the Gozitans. The people of Mosta insist that their dome beats that of Xewkija when measured by volume rather than by height *(see p38)*.

"Clapham Junction" Cart Ruts, Msierah

5 Mysterious Bronze Age grooves have been found across Malta, but this is the most dramatic site, with thousands of tracks etched into the rock on a wild and beautiful plateau near the Dingli Cliffs. Although they are called cart ruts, no one really knows what they are *(see p35)*.

The Miracle at Mosta

A congregation of about three hundred had gathered for mass on the afternoon of 9 April 1942 when a German bomb pierced the lofty Mosta Dome, clattered onto the floor and skidded through the church. Unbelievably, the bomb didn't explode, and the Maltese have always chosen to interpret this as a miracle. You can see a replica of the bomb, along with some period photographs of the church during World War II, in a small museum which is part of the church.

Verdala Palace and Buskett Gardens

Visible from much of southern Malta, the crenellated turrets of Verdala Palace seem to float above dense forest. The palace was built as a summer residence for Grand Master Hughes de Verdalle in 1588, but it is now used by the Maltese president and is not open to the public. The forest, known as the Buskett Gardens *(see p43)*, constitutes Malta's only real woodlands, with leafy paths and picnic areas. ✎ Triq Il-Buskett • Map C5

Palazzo Parisio

Palazzo Parisio, Naxxar

This aristocratic palace was originally built for the popular Portuguese Grand Master Manoel de Vilhena *(see p36)* in 1733. At the end of the 19th century, it was bought by a noble Maltese family, who completely transformed their new acquisition. The result was an opulent mansion which combined all the latest fashions (including the telephone) with superb local craftsmanship. Don't miss the beautiful formal Baroque gardens, elegant and particularly lovely in spring *(see pp18–19)*.

Fort Madliena, Madliena

This sturdy, pentagonal fort was one of four built to defend the Victoria Lines. The 12-km (7-mile) walls and their fortifications were built by the British in the late 19th century and completely spanned the island east to west. Fort Madliena still commands the surrounding countryside from its lofty promontory on Malta's northeastern coast, and is the only one of the four open to visitors. Best of all are the views out over the old fortified walls, which spill down a steep gorge – overgrown now but still surprisingly intact. The fort is run by the St John Rescue Corps, which puts on guided tours at weekends. ✎ Map D3 • 2133 5524 • Open for guided visits only, 2:30pm and 3:30pm Sat

The Three Villages (Balzan, Lija and Attard)

These villages consist of three neighbouring settlements. At first glance, they blend blandly into the suburban sprawl that extends dustily over much of Malta. And yet their historic kernels contain some of the island's most desirable addresses. Safe from the Ottomans after the Great Siege of 1565, the Maltese began a

Fort Madliena

building boom, and the smartest villas and palaces were built in the Three Villages. The villages grew, and their boundaries merged, but they remained fashionable under the British and even today. A wander through these affluent, leafy streets brings you face to face with medieval parish churches and Baroque villas, English-style mansions and contemporary luxury apartment blocks. The loveliest church is the 1613 parish church at Attard, built by Tommaso Dingli and probably the finest Renaissance church on the islands. ◈ *Map D4*

10 San Anton Palace Gardens, Attard

These quiet and beautiful gardens are tucked away in San Anton, a hushed suburb of Attard. The gardens are attached to a splendid summer palace, built by Grand Master Antoine de Paule in the 1620s. The palace is now the official residence of the President of Malta and is closed to visitors, but a section of the palace gardens has been open to the public since 1882. They are at their most beautiful in spring, when the carefully manicured flowerbeds and elegantly arranged flowerpots explode in a riot of colour and scent. A small aviary contains peacocks and other exotic birds. ◈ *De Paule Ave, San Anton • Map D4 • Open 8am–dusk*

A Walk around Mdina

Morning

🕐 Enter Mdina through the main gate. Almost immediately on the right, you'll pass the **Palazzo Vilhena** (now the Natural History Museum; *see p16*). Peek at the patio by the main entrance (the museum itself is rather dull) before heading to the sumptuous **Xara Palace Hotel** *(see p113)* for coffee in a marvellous 18th-century palace. Continue up narrow Triq San Pawl until you reach the entrance to **St Paul's Cathedral** *(see p38)*, one of the most beautiful ecclesiastical buildings in Malta. Across the square, the **Cathedral Museum** *(see p41)* is an enjoyably chaotic treasure trove of unexpected delights. The highlight is the collection of magnificent Dürer engravings and woodcuts. Linger over lunch at **Bacchus** *(see p57)*.

Afternoon

Walk up **Triq Villegaignon** *(see p17)*, Mdina's grandest street, lined with elaborate churches and graceful palaces with worn stone escutcheons. Look out for the **Casa Testaferrata** on the right; the French governor was thrown from the balcony of this noble house in 1798, when the Maltese decided they had had enough of the greedy French troops. Farther up, the **Palazzo Falzon** is the best-preserved medieval palace in Mdina. Triq Villegaignon opens up into the **Pjazza Tas-Sur** (Bastion Square), where breathtaking views unfold of the whole of central Malta. Close by, the open-air **Fontanella Tea Gardens** *(see p89)* are a good stop for tea and cakes.

Left **Wignacourt aqueduct** Centre **Ta' Qali Crafts Village** Right **Mk IX Spitfire, Malta Aviation Museum**

Best of the Rest

1 Limestone Heritage, Siġġiewi

Malta is one huge quarry, the source of the stone that built the ancient temples and the city of Valletta. Audiovisual displays at this former quarry tell the story. ◎ Triq Mons M. Azzopardi • Map C5 • 2146 4931 • Open Mon–Fri 9am–3pm, Sat 9am–12 noon, Sun 9–11:30am • Adm charge • www.limestoneheritage.com

2 Ta' Qali Crafts Village

Refurbished Nissen huts on a disused airfield showcase traditional Maltese crafts, from glass-blowing to pottery. There are demonstrations, and the prices are reasonable. ◎ Ta' Qali airfield, between Mdina and Attard • Map C4 • Open Mon–Sat 9am–4pm • Free

3 Malta Aviation Museum

A fascinating collection of vintage aircraft, including a WWII Spitfire and Hurricane (see p53).

4 Qormi

An otherwise humdrum town, Qormi has two claims to fame: it makes the best bread in the islands, and it has one of the largest and most flamboyant Baroque churches, the Church of St George. ◎ Map D4

5 Birkirkara

One of the largest Maltese towns since medieval times, Birkirkara preserves a small and atmospheric old quarter and a pair of handsome parish churches. ◎ Map D4

6 Wignacourt Aqueduct, Attard

This 16-km (10-mile) aqueduct funded in 1610 by Grand Master Wignacourt was still bringing water from Rabat to Valletta more than two centuries later. A large section survives in Attard. ◎ Triq Peter Paul Rubens • Map C4

7 Victoria Lines

The Great Fault, a dramatic natural fissure, cuts across Malta east–west. It is a natural line of defence, which the British built on to form the Victoria Lines. It's great walking country. ◎ Map B4

8 Fort Mosta

One of four British-built forts which guarded the Victoria Lines, this well-preserved example of fine Victorian engineering was completed in 1879 but never saw battle. ◎ Map C3 • Closed to the public

9 San Pawl Tat-Tarġa (Cart Ruts)

These strange grooves cut into stone have puzzled historians for centuries. If they are cart ruts, why do they run off the edge of cliffs? If not, what are they? ◎ San Pawl Tat-Tarġa, near Naxxar • Map C3

10 Żebbuġ

A shabby triumphal arch hints at Żebbuġ's former glory. Its vast parish church, designed by Gerolamo Cassar, architect of St John's, Valletta, has fared better, and its elegant spires float above the town. ◎ Map C5

Price Categories

For a three course
meal for one with half
a bottle of wine (or
equivalent meal), taxes
and extra charges.

€ under 5 Lm/€12
€€ 5–10 Lm/€12–24
€€€ 10–15 Lm/€24–36
€€€€ 15–20 Lm/€36–48
€€€€€ over 20 Lm/€48

De Mondion restaurant, Xara Palace Hotel, Mdina

TOP 10 Restaurants and Cafés

1 Fontanella Tea Gardens, Mdina
Perched on the ramparts behind Mdina's cathedral, Fontanella has spectacular views. Delicious tea and cakes are served in an ivy-draped courtyard or out on the terrace. Service is famously bad. ❧ *1 Triq Is-Sur • Map C4 • 2145 0208*

2 Medina, Mdina
Medina's thick stone walls have stood for almost a thousand years. In summer, you can dine under vines in the courtyard. The menu fuses French, Italian and Mediterranean cuisines. ❧ *7 Triq Is-Salib Imqaddes • Map C4 • 2145 4004 • Closed Sun, Mon–Sat L • €€€€*

3 Stazzjon, Rabat
Rabat's old railway station is now a delightful little café. You can dine in the waiting room or out on the platform, and order drinks at the ticket office. ❧ *Triq Mtarfa • Map C4 • 2145 1717*

4 De Mondion, Mdina
One of Malta's few genuine gastronomic temples, De Mondion is located in one of its most beautiful hotels, the Xara Palace. Eat superb French and Mediterranean food in romantic surroundings. ❧ *Xara Palace Hotel • Map C4 • 2145 0560 • Closed Sun, Mon–Sat L • €€€€€*

5 Bacchus, Mdina
This magnificent stone palace boasts a vaulted dining room, a panoramic terrace and exquisite gardens *(see p57)*.

6 Lord Nelson, Mosta
Set in a charming 300-year-old building, the Lord Nelson has a short menu of Maltese dishes with a modern twist. ❧ *278 Main Street • Map C4 • 2143 2590 • Closed Sun, Mon, Tue–Sat L, 3 weeks in Aug, 1 week after New Year and Easter • €€€€*

7 Rickshaw, Attard
One of several restaurants in this smart hotel, the Rickshaw offers Thai, Balinese, Japanese and other Asian cuisines. A popular spot for romantic dining. ❧ *Corinthia Palace Hotel, De Paule Avenue, San Anton • Map C4 • 2144 0301 • Closed Sun, Mon–Sat L • €€€€*

8 Bobbyland
Staggering views over the Dingli Cliffs are this country restaurant's main attraction. The food is simple country fare like rabbit and lamb. Avoid weekends, when it's jam-packed. ❧ *Triq I-Irdum, Dingli • Map B5 • 2145 2895 • Closed Mon • €€€*

9 Buskett Roadhouse
Best take a picnic to Buskett Woods. Otherwise, this large family restaurant offers hefty portions but little charm. ❧ *Buskett Gardens • Map C5 • 2145 4233 • €€*

10 Ir-Razzett l'Antik, Qormi
Staff in traditional dress serve 18th-century cuisine at this friendly restaurant in a historic building filled with antiques and curios. ❧ *Valley Road • Map D4 • 2147 0221 • Closed L, Tue D • €€*

In Jan 2008, Malta abandons the Maltese lira (Lm) and adopts the euro (€); the price categories above refer to both currencies.

Ħaġar Qim and Mnajdra Temples

Around Southern Malta

SOUTHERN MALTA BOASTS the island's most exceptional ancient site in the underground necropolis of the Ħal Saflieni Hypogeum, as well as the two most picturesque temples at Ħaġar Qim and Mnajdra. It also has the prettiest fishing harbour (Marsaxlokk), most dramatic cave (the Blue Grotto) and loveliest medieval chapels (Old St Gregory's and Ħal Millieri). Quiet, low-key resorts such as Marsaskala are good for families, and there's some fine hiking and bathing to be done in the Delimara Peninsula. This southern corner of the island is rural and tranquil, with patchwork fields defined by old stone walls. Each peaceful little village has its own ornate Baroque church, which is the centre of village life, and is best seen when lit up for the village festa.

 Sights

1 Ħaġar Qim and Mnajdra Temples
2 Ghar Dalam Cave and Museum, Birżebbuġa
3 Ħal Saflieni Hypogeum
4 Tarxien Temples
5 Marsaxlokk
6 Marsaskala
7 Blue Grotto, Wied Iż-Żurrieq
8 Ghar Lapsi
9 Delimara Peninsula
10 Chapel of Ħal Millieri, Żurrieq

Marsaxlokk

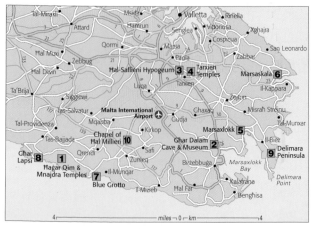

Preceding pages View of Senglea from Vittoriosa

Haġar Qim and Mnajdra Temples

These two beautiful temples emerge from a sea of poppies on a clifftop overlooking the Mediterranean. Overgrown fields with tumbling limestone walls stretch in every direction, and the lonely location – so unusual on the cramped little island of Malta – only

Tarxien Temples

adds to the charged atmosphere. The temples are made of soft globigerina limestone, and wind and time have eroded the stone into lacy shapes. Both temples are extraordinary and fascinating; Haġar Qim is the largest and most complex, while Mnajdra seems to have been designed to act as a calendar built of stone (see pp14–15).

Għar Dalam Cave and Museum, Birżebbuġa

Għar Dalam is a unique cave and prehistoric site, where a spectacular collection of 180,000-year-old bones belonging to long-extinct animals – which included dwarf hippopotamuses and dwarf elephants – were deposited at the end of the Ice Age. You can visit the cave, plus the small museum that is attached, where two rooms display the main finds of the palaeontologists (see p35).

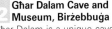

Figurine from the Hal Saflieni Hypogeum

Għar Dalam Museum

Hal Saflieni Hypogeum

Malta's most astonishing ancient treasure, this vast, 5,000-year-old underground cemetery was hewn by hand from the rock. It was here that the famous sculpture of the "Sleeping Lady" was found (see p40). If you see only one megalithic site in Malta, make it this one – but be sure to book your ticket well ahead (see pp22–3).

Tarxien Temples

The Tarxien Temples are the most complex of Malta's temple sites. Elaborate decorative objects have been found here, including huge statues of the so-called "Fat Ladies" – fertility goddesses. Sadly, the site is overlooked by drab apartment buildings in one of the islands' least prepossessing towns, but there are plans to improve things with a glassy new visitors' centre which will also protect the ruins (see p34).

Marsaxlokk

This is Malta's prettiest and most authentic fishing port. The delightful harbour is filled with bobbing, brightly coloured luzzus. Cobalt-blue fishing nets are spread out along the quays, and countless fish restaurants surround the bay (see pp20–21).

The Not-So-Great Great White Shark

Little Wied Iż-Żurrieq made international news in 1987, when a local fisherman landed a gigantic great white shark. Locals claimed that it was 7m (23ft) long, which would have made it one of the biggest great whites ever discovered. (If you hear this story from your fisherman-guide on the way to the Blue Grotto, it's likely that it will have grown another metre or two.) Unfortunately, after scientists did tests with photographs, the shark's size was eventually revealed to be around 5–5.5 m (17–18 ft) – big, certainly, but no larger than many other great whites discovered in the Mediterranean.

Marsaskala

An overgrown fishing village that still retains its fishing fleet, Marsaskala has become one of the biggest resorts at the southern end of the island. Despite its size, it retains a sleepy charm, and even in July and August, when the town is crammed to the gills, it's still quieter and less frenzied than the northern resorts. Families stroll along the harbour front during the evening *passeggiata*, watching the fishermen mending their nets, before heading to one of the area's excellent seafood restaurants. For swimming and snorkelling, walk around the headland to nearby St Thomas's Bay, which is extremely popular with the Maltese although not especially attractive. ◈ *Map F5*

7 Blue Grotto, Wied Iż-Żurrieq

At the tiny cove of Wied Iż-Żurrieq, a straggle of café-bars and tourist shops have sprung up to cater for the streams of visitors on their way to see the fabled Blue Grotto. Walk along the cliff path or take a boat ride into the massive cave (see p43).

8 Għar Lapsi

A natural lido formed by a rock pool scooped from the cliff, Għar Lapsi sounds much prettier than it is. The setting is quiet and attractive, but the pools are cursed with a coating of slimy seaweed and old rubbish. In spite of this, the Maltese adore Għar Lapsi and come in droves during the summer months, when the lively family atmosphere lends it a certain charm. Watching the comings and goings of the fishermen who also use the cove is a pleasant way to spend an afternoon. A couple of restaurants overlook the lido, and offer panoramic views over the coastline. ◈ *Map C6*

9 Delimara Peninsula

This finger of land is the site of a huge and unsightly power station. Yet, remarkably, the Delimara Peninsula is one of the prettiest corners in all Malta.

Marsaskala

Blue Grotto

Neat vegetable and flower plots are interspersed with stretches of wilder country with undulating fields, and there are wonderful swimming holes. The best of them is the pretty little cove of St Peter's Pool *(see p46)*, where the limestone cliffs have been eroded into ice-cream curves and the water is impossibly blue. There's another good spot for a swim at the very end of the peninsula, where the diving is particularly good. ◈ *Map F6*

🔟 Chapel of Ħal Millieri, Żurrieq

This tiny, stone-built chapel near the tranquil little town of Żurrieq is shaded by lofty pines. It was built on the remnants of an older chapel and was consecrated in 1480. It was the parish church of Casal Millieri, an ancient village that existed even before Roman times but which has long since disappeared, leaving just the lonely chapel in its leafy grove. Inside, the arched vault is divided into five bays, each beautifully decorated with frescoes depicting various saints, including St George enthusiastically finishing off the dragon. These frescoes were buried under layers of whitewash for many years and their bottom sections are irredeemably damaged. ◈ *Map D6 • 2122 0358 • Open first Sun of month 9:30am–12 noon, or by appointment • Free • www. dinlarthelwa.org*

A Tour around Southern Malta

Morning

Get to **Wied Iż-Żurrieq** nice and early to avoid the queues for the **Blue Grotto**. It's at its best in the bright morning sunshine when the water is an extraordinary electric blue. After the boat trip, head to **Marsaxlokk** – a tricky drive because there are few signs. (Take the Kirkop–Gudja–Għaxaq route to avoid getting lost in the Ħal Far industrial estate.) Once in the charming fishing port of Marsaxlokk, go for a stroll around the harbour and admire the multicoloured *luzzu* bobbing in the bay, before enjoying an alfresco lunch. For fresh seafood and harbour views, get a table on the water's edge at **Pisces** *(see p97)* but remember to book it well in advance.

Afternoon

After lunch, drive (or take a stroll) out to **St Peter's Pool** on the **Delimara Peninsula**. Fishermen will also ferry passengers from Marsaxlokk harbour to the little cove. Spend a couple of hours sunbathing and swimming in the pool's transparent waters. Then hop into the car for the short drive to **Marsaskala**, where you should just be in time to join the evening *passeggiata* around the harbour. Stop for a drink in one of the seafront cafés before pondering where to have dinner. To push the boat out, go for Grabiel *(see p57)*, which many consider to be the best seafood restaurant on the island. For something less upmarket but reliably good, try the Fisherman's Rest at St Thomas's Bay *(see p97)*.

Left **Old St Gregory's** Middle **St Catherine's** Right **Chapel of Our Lady of Graces**

TOP 10 Churches and Chapels

1 Chapel of Our Lady of Providence, near Siġġiewi

This dainty octagonal chapel is usually closed, but through a window you may spot a cannon ball said to date from the Great Siege (1565). ◈ *2 km (1 mile)from Siġġiewi on Għar Lapsi road • Map C5 • 2146 0827 • Open for Mass 1 Sep*

2 St Nicholas, Siġġiewi

Designed by the prestigious Baroque architect Lorenzo Gafa, this enormous, stately church dominates Siġġiewi's central square. ◈ *Pjazza San Nicolas • Map C5 • 2146 0827 • Festa last Sun in Jun*

3 Chapel of Our Lady of Graces, Żabbar

The pink, frilly domes of this Baroque church, also called the Żabbar Sanctuary, dominate the town's traffic-blighted old centre. A museum contains sailors' ex-votos. ◈ *Triq Is-Santwarju • Map E5 • 2182 4383 • Festa first Sun after 8 Sep*

4 Our Lady of the Annunciation, Tarxien

This august 17th-century parish church sits serenely at the centre of a confusing maze of narrow streets. ◈ *Triq Il-Kbira • Map E5 • 2182 8153 • Festa fifth Sun after Easter*

5 St Catherine's, Żejtun

The grandiose 17th-century parish church dominates this languid village. Designed by Lorenzo Gafa, it overlooks the square. ◈ *Main square • Map E5 • 2169 4563 • Festa Jun (date varies)*

6 Old St Gregory's, Żejtun

Built in 1436, this simple whitewashed structure, topped with a shallow dome and belltower, is one of the oldest surviving churches in Malta. ◈ *Triq San Girgor • Map E5 • 2167 7187 • Open for Mass weekends • Festa first Wed after Easter*

7 Bir Miftuh Chapel, Gudja

This graceful 15th-century church dedicated to St Mary of the Open Well now stands too close for comfort to the runways of Malta's international airport. Inside are the faded remnants of 17th-century murals. ◈ *Gudja • Map E5 • 2122 0358 • Festa 15 Aug*

8 St George's Chapel, Birżebbuġa

Built by the Knights in 1683, this is the only fortified church on the coast. ◈ *St George's Bay, Borġ In-Nadur • Map E6 • Closed to the public*

9 St Mary, Qrendi

Lorenzo Gafa transformed an older building into this handsome Baroque parish church in pretty Qrendi. The rivalry between it and that of neighbouring Mqabba is legendary. ◈ *Triq Il-Knisja • Map D6 • 2164 9395 • Festa 15 Aug*

10 Christ the King, Paola

Giuseppe D'Amato's modern church overlooks Paola's dreary suburban sprawl. D'Amato was also architect of the huge church in Xewkija, Gozo *(see p39)*. ◈ *Pjazza de Paule • Map E5 • 2169 5022*

Price Categories

For a three course meal for one with half a bottle of wine (or equivalent meal), taxes and extra charges.

€	under 5 Lm/€12
€€	5–10 Lm/€12–24
€€€	10–15 Lm/€24–36
€€€€	15–20 Lm/€36–48
€€€€€	over 20 Lm/€48

Fisherman's Rest

Restaurants and Cafés

1 Fisherman's Rest, St Thomas's Bay
A friendly, family-run beachfront restaurant surrounded by fishing shacks, this is known for its fresh fish and modest prices.
◈ St Thomas's Bay • Map F5 • 2163 2049 • Closed Sun, Mon, Tue–Sat L • €€

2 Ir-Rizzu, Marsaxlokk
Fresh fish is the speciality at this great family-run restaurant overlooking the magnificent harbour. Book for Sunday lunch after the quayside fish market.
◈ 52 Xatt Is-Sajjieda • Map E5 • 2165 1569 • Closed public hols • €€€

3 Blue Creek Bar & Restaurant, Għar Lapsi
This smart, family-friendly spot looks out over the sea and the lido formed by a rocky inlet. It also has an inexpensive snack menu. ◈ Għar Lapsi • Map C6 • 2146 2800 • Closed Tue • €€€

4 Is-Sajjied Bar & Restaurant, Marsaxlokk
Another of Marsaxlokk's fine seafood restaurants, this has attractive nautical decor and a breezy terrace for summer dining. ◈ Xatt Is-Sajjieda • Map E5 • 2165 2549 • Closed Mon • €€€

5 Tal-Familja, Marsaskala
This spacious restaurant with rustic decor is great for local fish and Maltese cuisine. Daily specials are chalked up on a blackboard. ◈ Triq Il-Gardiel • Map F5 • 2163 2161 • Closed Mon • €€€

6 Pisces, Marsaxlokk
A long-standing stalwart of Marsaxlokk's dining scene, Pisces offers moderately priced seafood, along with Italian and Maltese fare. The glass-and-marble dining room is smarter than the slightly scruffy entrance suggests. ◈ 89 Xatt Is-Sajjieda • Map E5 • 2165 4956 • Closed Wed • €€

7 La Favorita, Marsaskala
This friendly restaurant comes highly recommended by locals for its seafood specialities and relaxed atmosphere. It's on the edge of town, near St Thomas's Bay. Book at weekends. ◈ Triq Il-Gardiel • Map F5 • 2163 4113 • Closed Mon • €€€

8 Jakarta, Marsaskala
A very popular oriental restaurant. Try the beef satay or roast Beijing duck, accompanied by one of the unusual Thai wines. ◈ Triq Il-Gardiel • Map F5 • 2163 3993 • Closed Sun D, Mon L, Tue, Wed–Sat L • €€€

9 Grabiel, Marsaskala
One of the islands' finest seafood restaurants – upmarket but not stuffy (see p57).

10 Prima, Żurrieq
Few villages in rural Malta have restaurants, but simple cafés and bakeries are always easy to find. This one is good for home-made pizza, pastizzi and wonderful bread. ◈ Main Street, near the church • Map D6

In Jan 2008, Malta abandons the Maltese lira (Lm) and adopts the euro (€); the price categories above refer to both currencies.

Left **The Citadel, Rabat/Victoria** Right **Calypso's Cave**

Around Gozo and Comino

GOZO IS SMALLER, GREENER AND QUIETER *than its big sister, Malta. At its heart is the Citadel, the miniature central capital of this miniature island. From this tiny walled metropolis, beautiful views extend across the plains and out to sea. Nearby, the Ġgantija temples are probably among the world's oldest freestanding monuments; gaze at these monumental ruins and ponder on the extraordinary culture that created them. The Gozitan coastline is breathtaking, particularly at Dwejra and the cliffs of Ta' Ċenċ, and the whole island is a walker's paradise. There's just one sandy beach, the ochre crescent of Ramla Bay, but countless coves and bays offer good spots for a dip. Smaller still, Comino is poised between Malta and Gozo; wild and largely empty, it boasts a population of four (or sometimes five). Droves of tourists descend daily to see the lovely Blue Lagoon, but in early morning and late afternoon the whole island returns to its habitual slumber.*

🔟 Sights

1. The Citadel, Rabat/Victoria
2. Ġgantija Temples
3. Dwejra
4. Santa Marija Bay, Comino
5. Blue Lagoon, Comino
6. Xewkija Rotunda
7. Ramla Bay
8. Calypso's Cave, Ramla Bay
9. Ta' Ċenċ Cliffs
10. Ta' Pinu Basilica, Gharb

Dwejra

For a good overview of Gozo's history, check out the Gozo 360° audiovisual show at the Citadel Theatre in Rabat/Victoria.

Ġgantija Temples

The Citadel, Rabat/Victoria

At the physical and spiritual heart of Gozo, this tiny walled city sits high on a rocky bluff, commanding views of virtually the whole island. A citadel has existed here since Roman times, but the current stucture was built in the 17th century after the previous walls were breached by the corsair Dragut Rais. Gozitans still refer to their capital as Rabat, even though it was officially renamed Victoria to celebrate the British Queen's Diamond Jubilee in 1897 (see pp24–5).

Ġgantija Temples

The huge, pale stones of Ġgantija have stood for more than five and a half millennia – over a thousand years longer than the pyramids of Egypt.

Despite its age, this temple complex is one of the best-preserved in the Maltese archipelago, with sturdy walls reaching up to 7 m (23 ft) in height (see p35).

Dwejra

Dwejra's sheer cliffs, curving bays, gigantic caves and entrancing rock formations combine to make it Gozo's most celebrated photo-opportunity. Although tourists gather in droves at the foot of the striking Azure Window (a rocky opening framing stunning views), it's possible to strike out along the cliff paths to enjoy the panorama in relative peace (see pp26–7).

Santa Marija Bay, Comino

There are two attractive bays, both with sought-after strips of sand, on the island of Comino, but this one is public while the other is private. Out of season you may well find you have it all to yourself (see p47).

Blue Lagoon, Comino

The main draw on Comino is the magical Blue Lagoon, the focus of innumerable daily boat cruises. Those staying on the island can enjoy it without the hordes of day-trippers (see p47).

Blue Lagoon, Comino

An underground burial chamber similar to the famous Ħal Saflieni Hypogeum (see pp22–3) is being excavated near the Ġgantija Temples. The early excavation notes for the Hypogeum were lost, so the careful exploration of the Xagħra Circle has enormous importance for archeologists seeking to understand the world of the Maltese temple-builders. This site was neither as large nor as lavishly decorated as Ħal Saflieni, but the ongoing excavation works have advanced understanding of prehistoric burial rites to a remarkable degree.

Xewkija Rotunda

Just as the Mosta Dome dominates much of the island of Malta, so the Xewkija Rotunda is visible from almost everywhere in Gozo. It is Europe's third-largest dome, although the people of Mosta still claim theirs is bigger. Architect Giuseppe D'Amato was inspired by the Basilica of Santa Maria Della Salute in Venice. His church is made of local limestone. It was begun in 1951 and took 20 years to build (see p39).

Ramla Bay

Ramla has Gozo's best beach, backed by gentle hills with tumbling terraces. It's also the only truly sandy beach on the island. Out of season, it feels like a corner of paradise, but at the height of the summer it can get unbearably crowded. Almost 2,000 years ago, a Roman villa was built on this idyllic spot. You can see the sparse remains close to the beach (see p47).

Calypso's Cave, Ramla Bay

In this lofty cave, carved out of the rock high above Ramla Bay, the love-sick nymph Calypso is said to have seduced Odysseus in Homer's epic *The Odyssey*. Get there by scrambling up the short but steep path which leads from the beachfront. (Ask in the café for directions.) Once at the entrance, you can stroll through the pretty manicured little garden to the lookout point to enjoy tremendous views. Steps lead down to the cave itself, which is disappointingly dank and rubbish-filled. If you do scramble all the way down, the rocks open onto the sea, framing more stunning views. Gazing out at the endless, cobalt sea, it's easy to imagine the nymph whispering sweet nothings to her reluctant lover.

⊗ Follow signs from Xagħra • Map E1
• Open 9am–dusk • Free

Ta' Ċenċ Cliffs

This stretch of wild cliffs, which plunge sheerly and terrifyingly into the sea below, is one of the most beautiful sights in Gozo. Go at dusk, when the cliffs are flushed pink by the setting sun. For centuries, bird-trappers swung down these cliffs in rough slings on ropes. Hunting and trapping are now banned, but few Maltese hunters

Ramla Bay

Get off the beaten track in the southeastern corner of Gozo, beyond Qala, where there's some fine hiking and quiet coves.

Ta' Ċenċ Cliffs

A Tour around Gozo

Morning

Set off early, so that you can arrive at the cliffs of **Dwejra** *(see pp26–7)* in time to enjoy them without the crowds. Take a boat ride through the **Inland Sea** through to the **Azure Window**. Take some time to stroll along the cliff paths and enjoy spectacular views of **Fungus Rock** and the rugged coastline. Drive to **Victoria** (which locals still call Rabat) to explore the lofty walled **citadel** *(see pp24–5)*. Don't miss the frothy Baroque **cathedral** and the excellent **Museum of Archaeology**. You can have a simple but delicious lunch of fresh bread and local cheese at Ta' Rikardu *(see p103)*.

Afternoon

After lunch, drive to nearby **Xagħra** to see the ancient **Ġgantija Temples**, in a beautiful setting overlooking a wide, green plain. The same ticket also gains admission to the **Ta' Kola Windmill** on the outskirts of the village. Head next to the village square, where one of the little café-bars should be open for a drink. If you have enough time, you could drive on for another 10 minutes to **Ramla Bay**, Gozo's best beach, for a refreshing dip. Then return to the other side of the island and make for Sannat, following the signs for **Ta' Ċenċ**. Spend an enjoyable hour strolling around these magnificent cliffs as dusk falls. Finally, you could dine on fresh fish at Sammy's *(see p103)*, on the water-front in **Mġarr Harbour**, finishing the day with a drink at the nearby Gleneagles Bar, which has a fantastic terrace overlooking the port.

seem to have taken note, and the local bird population has suffered terribly as a result. Nonetheless, numerous bird species continue to make the Ta' Ċenċ cliffs their home *(see p42)*.

Ta' Pinu Basilica, Għarb

The Ta' Pinu Basilica is Gozo's most important place of pilgrimage. Our Lady of Ta' Pinu is credited with miraculous healing powers, and numerous ex-votos (including crutches and artificial limbs) attest to prayers being answered. The huge modern church (which was completed in 1931) retains a section of the original 19th-century chapel where, in 1883, a local woman is reputed to have seen a vision of Our Lady *(see p39)*.

Ta' Pinu Basilica, Għarb

Left **Mġarr harbour** Right **St George's Basilica**

Best of the Rest

Folklore Museum, Għarb
An engaging little museum in one of Gozo's prettiest, least spoilt villages. It has a collection of tools, costumes, paintings and curiosities typical of rural Gozitan life. ⊗ 99 Church Square • Map D1 • 2156 1929 • Open 9am–4pm Mon–Sat, 9am–1pm Sun • Adm charge

St George's Basilica, Rabat/Victoria
Known as the "Golden Church" for its dazzling, gilded interior, this sumptuous Baroque edifice was designed by Vittorio Cassar and completed in 1673. Inside is a curious statue of St George carved from a single tree. ⊗ Pjazza San Ġorġ • Map D2 • 2155 6377 • Open for Mass daily • Free

Ta' Kola Windmill, Xagħra
Built in 1725, this is the only survivor of twelve windmills built by the Knights. All kinds of objects related to traditional Maltese crafts have been gathered here in an interesting little museum. ⊗ Triq Bambina • Map E1 • 2156 1071 • Open 9am–5pm daily • Adm charge • www.heritagemalta.org

Ta' Dbieġi Crafts Village, Għarb
Gozo's craft village is not as big as Malta's but is still convenient for souvenir-shopping. There are demonstrations of traditional crafts, and it's a good place to pick up Gozitan woollen jumpers and rugs. ⊗ Triq San Lawrenz • Map D1 • Open 9:30am–5pm Mon–Sat

Xlendi Bay
This once-beautiful bay, between silvery cliffs, has been spoilt by careless development, but it remains one of Gozo's most popular resorts (see p47).

Marsalforn
Once a tiny fishing village, Marsalforn is now a sprawling, but still low-key, resort on Gozo's northern coast (see p47).

Salt Pans, Reqqa Point
Hundreds of salt pans indent the soft limestone near Marsalforn, forming a surreal landscape of strange, natural beauty (see p42).

San Blas Bay
This beautiful little bay, with its strip of ochre sand, is hard to reach (you'll need to scramble down a steep footpath), but it's well worth it (see p42).

Mġarr Harbour
Guarded by a fortress and hemmed in by cliffs, the focus of the village is still the salty old port, full of colourful *luzzus* and vivid blue fishing nets. ⊗ Map F2

Comino Tower (St Mary's Tower), Comino
It wasn't until 1618 that Comino got long-promised fortifications to protect it from pirates. This tower still guards the island's southwestern approaches, and has been newly restored to its former glory. ⊗ Map F3

Local bread, Gozitan cheese, fresh tomatoes and some local wine makes a great picnic.

Price Categories

For a three course meal for one with half a bottle of wine (or equivalent meal), taxes and extra charges.

€ under 5 Lm/€12
€€ 5–10 Lm/€12–24
€€€ 10–15 Lm/€24–36
€€€€ 15–20 Lm/€36–48
€€€€€ over 20 Lm/€48

Zeppi's Pub

TOP 10 Restaurants and Cafés

1 Gesther, Xagħra
For old-fashioned Maltese cooking, nowhere beats this simple restaurant, tucked away in a quiet Gozitan village *(see p57)*.

2 Il-Kcina Tal-Barrakka (Sammy's), Mġarr Harbour
This harbourside eaterie is one of the best places to try fresh fish. It's run by the same owners as the fabulous Gleneagles Bar nearby. Book well in advance. ◈ *28 Manoel de Vilhena Street • Map F2 • 2155 6543 • Closed Nov–Apr; May–Oct: Mon, Tue–Sun L • €€€*

3 Ta' Frenc, Gozo
This exceptional restaurant, in a stylishly restored old farmhouse, is often considered the best in all Malta *(see p56)*.

4 La Stanza Restaurant & Bar, Rabat/Victoria
An endearingly eccentric restaurant and bar in an old farmhouse beneath the citadel, this has a pretty garden and a roof terrace. The Maltese and Mediterranean menu includes weekly specials. ◈ *56 Triq I-Imgħallem • Map D2 • 2155 5953 • Closed L daily • €€*

5 It-Tmun, Rabat/Victoria
A coolly elegant restaurant decorated with contemporary art, this is popular with a well-heeled local crowd. Go for the six-course "tasting menu". ◈ *Triq Europe • Map D2 • 2156 6667 • Closed Mon–Wed L, Thu, Fri–Sat L • €€€€*

6 Jeffrey's, Għarb
A perennial favourite, this rustically furnished village restaurant serves up delicious and authentic local cuisine at bargain prices *(see p56)*.

7 Ta' Rikardu, Rabat/Victoria
Conveniently located right next to the cathedral in the Citadel, this rustic little spot serves delicious local bread, cheese and wine *(see p56)*.

8 Oleander, Xagħra
An old-fashioned country restaurant on the main square of a charming village, Oleander serves sturdy Maltese favourites such as *fenek* (rabbit) and traditional soups. Booking is essential. ◈ *10 Pjazza Victoria • Map E1 • 2155 7230 • Closed Mon • €€€*

9 Comino Hotel, Comino
It's best to bring a picnic and find your own quiet corner if you want to avoid the crowds on Comino. This hotel has the only restaurant on the island, offering reasonable Mediterranean cuisine. ◈ *San Niklaw Bay • Map F2 • 2152 9821 • Closed Nov–Feb • €€€*

10 Zeppi's Pub, Qala
This attractive village pub offers a great range of imaginative lunchtime snacks, including salads, omelettes and *croques monsieurs*. The art gallery upstairs also sells wonderful gifts. ◈ *St Joseph Square • Map F2 • 2156 0069 • Closed Mon L • €*

In Jan 2008, Malta abandons the Maltese lira (Lm) and adopts the euro (€); the price categories above refer to both currencies.

STREETSMART

MALTA'S TOP 10

Streetsmart

Left **Valletta Airport** Right **A Valletta bus**

Getting to and Around Malta

1 By Air
Malta International Airport is at Luqa, about 8 km (5 miles) from Valletta. The national airline Air Malta connects with more than 50 major cities. A few other big carriers, including Alitalia, Lufthansa and British Airways also fly to Luqa, but so far no budget airlines fly to Malta. ✆ Map D5 • 2124 9600 • www.maltairport.com

2 Charters and Packages
Many charter flights and flight/hotel packages are available – especially in the summer season, but deals are available year-round. Flight-only deals are hard to come by in July and August.

3 Cruises
Valletta is a stopover on many Mediterranean cruises, with a modern terminal right on the beautiful Grand Harbour. The approach to Valletta by ship is unforgettable: the view has barely changed in five centuries. Smaller ships may dock at Xlendi Harbour, Gozo.

4 Sailing
Malta's spectacular harbours and enchanting coves have attracted sailors for thousands of years. The two biggest marinas are in Marsamxett Harbour, between Valletta and Sliema. The Maritime Authority, Customs Office and Royal Malta

Yacht Club are all nearby. Pleasure craft may anchor for the night in all bays and inlets except at Filfla Island. ✆ Maltese Maritime Authority, Marina Pinto, Valletta • 2122 2203 • www. mma.gov.mt

5 Getting Around by Bus
Many of Malta's much-photographed snub-nosed buses date back half a century. They are rather slow, but fares are cheap and routes fairly comprehensive. Buses on Malta are yellow with an orange stripe; most journeys begin at Valletta. Rabat/Victoria is the main terminus on Gozo, where the buses are grey with a scarlet stripe. ✆ Valletta bus terminal, City Gate • Gozo bus terminal, Main City Gate, Rabat/Victoria

6 Getting Around by Ferry
Gozo Channel Company operates a car and passenger ferry between Ċirkewwa (Malta) and Mġarr Harbour (Gozo). A passenger-only ferry links Sliema and Valletta. The Comino Hotel runs a small ferry to Comino, but local boat tours make regular runs to the Blue Lagoon from Mġarr Harbour and Ċirkewwa.

7 Getting Around: Boat Excursions
One of the most enjoyable ways to see the Maltese islands is by boat. Some of the prettiest coves and

most dramatic stretches of coastline can only be reached by sea. Many tour operators are based in Sliema or Xlendi (Gozo).

8 Getting Around by Car
A car is invaluable to get off the beaten track. But be prepared for pot-holed roads, decrepit vehicles and Maltese drivers' blithe disregard for speed limits and other road-users. All major rental firms are at the airport; local firms are cheaper and usually very reliable.

9 Getting Around by Helicopter
A convenient helicopter service links Luqa airport in Malta with Xewkija Heliport in Gozo, taking about 15 minutes. Flights are coordinated with international arrivals and departures. Weekend and one-day fly-drive deals are available. ✆ Gozo Heliport, Xewkija • Map E2 • 2155 7905 • www.airgozo.com

10 Getting Around on Foot
Despite the development that has mushroomed across the islands, Malta still has a few unspoilt corners with spellbinding scenery. Hiking is popular and best in spring, when flowers carpet the fields and the islands are cooler and quieter. There are several good walking guides; check them out in Sapienza's Bookshop (see p64).

Left **Dual-language street sign** Right **Tourist Information Office**

TOP 10 General Information

1 Climate
Malta has a typically Mediterranean climate: hot, sunny summers, mild winters, and low rainfall all year round. In spring and autumn the islands can be affected by the *sirocco*, a scorching wind that blows in from Africa. The bitingly cold *gregale* brings storms. July and August are the hottest months, September and October the wettest.

2 When to Go
Malta's high season runs from late June to September. If you can, avoid the crowds and heat of July and August; in September and June the islands are warm but less crowded. Spring is beautiful, before the intense greens and the vivid blooms of wild flowers give way to dusty browns and greys.

3 Passports and Visas
Malta joined the EU in 2004. Citizens of most European countries, the USA, Canada, Australia and New Zealand need no visa for stays of up to 90 days. A visa is needed for longer stays; get one from a high commission, embassy or consulate – check the Malta Ministry of Foreign Affairs website. ✆ *www.foreign.gov.mt*

4 Embassies and Consulates
Maltese embassies and consulates can supply information about visiting, studying, working, or retiring in Malta. The Maltese foreign ministry website *(see above)* has a directory of offices.

5 Tourist Offices Abroad
The helpful Malta Tourism Authority (MTA) is a useful first port-of-call when planning your trip. It has offices in Australia and many European countries including the UK. Addresses are listed on its website. ✆ *www. mta.com.mt*

6 Tourist Offices in Malta
Malta's main tourist information office is just inside Valletta's City Gate. The friendly staff can provide information on everything from bus routes to local *festas*. There are also offices in St Julian's and Rabat/Victoria (Gozo), and a booth at the airport.

7 Internet Information
The official tourist website, *www.visitmalta. com*, has comprehensive information on everything to see and do, and a useful interactive map. For information on *festas* and other events, check out *www.maltafestivals. com*. For affectionate insights into the islands, try *www.my-malta.com*. The website *www.gozo. com* provides a wealth of information on Gozo. The leading newspaper, *The Times of Malta*, has an informative website: *www.timesofmalta.com*.

8 Language
Maltese and English are the official languages. Maltese is closely related to Arabic, but uses the Latin alphabet with a few special marks *(see p126)*. You'll hear it spoken everywhere, but virtually everyone can speak English. Almost all of the street signs are in Maltese, but most shops and businesses use the English version in advertising. All road signs are in English.

9 Time Differences
Malta keeps Central European Time (CET), an hour ahead of GMT, but (as elsewhere in Europe) the clocks go forward one hour in summer. It is one hour ahead of the UK, six hours ahead of New York and nine hours ahead of California.

10 Local Customs
The Maltese are devout Catholics. Dress suitably when entering a church (no shorts or strappy tops), and behave respectfully – expect to be admonished by a tutting usher. Topless sunbathing is prohibited on public beaches, but tolerated on private ones. Unofficial car park attendants expect a tip (50 cents average) but it's not compulsory.

Left **Village police station** Right **Valletta pharmacy**

Security and Health

1 Emergency Numbers

In an emergency, dial 112 for the police, fire brigade or ambulance. To report a traffic accident that doesn't need emergency services, call local wardens on 2132 0202. For non-urgent matters, contact police headquarters (see below).

2 Police

Every town and village has its own police station, easily spotted by the blue lantern outside in traditional British style. National police wear blue uniforms and should be contacted to report a crime. Police headquarters are in Floriana (Malta) and Rabat/Victoria (Gozo). Green-uniformed traffic wardens are responsible for road safety. Ⓝ Pjazza Vicenzo Buġeja, Floriana • 2294 0000 • Triq Ir-Repubblika, Rabat/Victoria • 2156 2040

3 Health Issues

By far the most common health problems for holiday-makers are caused by excessive sun. Always use sunscreen, drink plenty of water, and wear a hat in the open. Take particular care with small children. The water is safe to drink but tastes unpleasant. Bottled water is widely available.

4 Prescriptions

Most well-known medicines are easy to get in Malta. If you may need a repeat prescription, it's best to bring a doctor's letter to avoid problems with customs or the pharmacist. Note the generic name, as well as the brand name, of any drugs you may need.

5 Pharmacies

Every town and village has one or more chemists, identified by a green cross sign. Most follow normal shop hours, closing for lunch, but display the name of a duty pharmacy that is open nearby. Pharmacists can usually advise on simple health problems.

6 Disabled Travellers

The Maltese islands are not ideally equipped for disabled travellers, although things are now slowly improving. Hotels and restaurants in older buildings have virtually no facilities for wheelchair-users, although the accommodating Maltese will usually try their best to help. All new hotels, restaurants and visitors' attractions provide good disabled facilities. Buses do not generally have wheelchair access.

7 Women Travellers

Women visitors will have no difficulties in Malta, where the locals are friendly, open and generous. Drunken tourists can be more annoying. There's very little violent crime and no real "no-go" areas. But be aware that the culture is deeply traditional and the Catholic Church still exerts a huge influence – divorce and abortion, for example, are still illegal.

8 Gay Travellers

Malta decriminalized homosexuality in 1973, but it remains a deeply traditional society. Gay travellers are welcomed with typical Maltese generosity, but there is virtually no gay "scene", with just one gay hotel (the Hotel Kappara in Sliema) and only a couple of gay bars. Ġnejna Bay and Fomm Ir-Riħ Bay (see p82) are gay-friendly. Ⓝ Hotel Kappara, Triq Wied Għollieqa • 21 33 43 67 • www.kappara.freeola.com

9 Insurance

All visitors are recommended to take out travel insurance. EU citizens should note that reciprocal agreements don't cover, for example, dentistry and repatriation, and the bureaucracy can be hard to untangle.

10 Crime

There is comparatively little crime in Malta. Watch out for bag-snatchers or pickpockets in crowded resorts or at the beach, and try to keep your bag strapped across you. Avoid leaving anything in an unattended car, and leave the glove compartment open to show that it is empty. Report any crime to the police immediately.

Left **Valletta post box** Centre **Valletta telephone box** Right **International newspaper**

Banking and Communications

Currency
The unit of currency is the Maltese Lira, often still called the "pound" and abbreviated Lm or £. It is divided into 100 cents. There are Lm20, Lm10, Lm5 and Lm2 notes, and Lm1, 50c, 25c, 10c, 5c, 2c and 1c coins. Malta is due to switch to the Euro on 1 Jan 2008.

Changing Money
Cash and traveller's cheques can be readily exchanged at banks, bureaux de change and most hotels (although hotels often offer poor rates and charge high commissions). Banks usually offer the best rates and can be found in all the larger towns and resorts. It may be cheapest to use a debit card to withdraw money from an ATM machine.

Banking Hours
Banks' opening hours vary slightly, but are usually 8:30am–12:30pm Mon–Fri and 8:30–11:30am on Sat. Some banks in larger towns and resorts may open one or two afternoons a week, but those in smaller towns often close on Saturday mornings in summer.

Cash Dispensers
There are plenty of cash machines (ATMs) throughout the islands, at least in the larger towns and resorts. Look for an illuminated sign bearing a bank logo. They accept major debit and credit cards 24 hours a day. Instructions are available in English, French, German, Italian and Maltese.

Credit Cards
Credit cards are accepted at most moderate to expensive hotels and restaurants, and at most shops. But few budget hotels, small guesthouses and shops, or cheaper cafés and restaurants take them; nor do many museums. Mastercard and Visa are the most widely accepted, American Express and Diners Club less so.

Post
The Maltese postal system is generally reliable. Most larger towns have post offices, which are usually open 7:30am–12:45pm Mon–Sat. Main branches, such as those in Valletta and Rabat/Victoria (Gozo), stay open until 4:30pm and are also open on Saturday mornings. Post boxes are bright red, an appealing British tradition.

Telephones
Telephone boxes – also often in British-style scarlet, but otherwise green or clear – are easy to find in most towns and resorts. Most use phone cards (called Telecards and available from newsagents for Lm2, Lm3, Lm4 or Lm5), although a few still accept coins. In many old-fashioned bars and cafés it's acceptable to use the phone for local calls, leaving usually 25c.

Internet Cafés
All larger towns and resorts have Internet cafés. They seem to pop up and disappear without warning, so check with a tourist office or try the local website *(see below)* for a list. Some phone boxes give Internet access. ◉ *www. internetcafe.com.mt*

Newspapers and Magazines
Malta's leading newspaper is *The Times*, which famously continued to publish every day of World War II. *The Independent* has a similar conservative stance but a lower circulation. Both are English-language. *In-Nazzjon* and *L-Orizzont* are the main Maltese-language papers. British and other European publications are widely available on the day of publication. ◉ *www.timesofmalta.com*

Television
There are three main local TV stations. One is publicly owned, another is owned by the Labour Party and the third by the Nationalist Party. There's also good reception of Italian channels. Cable and satellite are hugely popular. Most hotels, even the most modest, have satellite television.

Left **Silversmith making filigree jewellery** Centre **Street market** Right **Self-catering apartment**

Eating, Shopping and Lodging

1 Restaurant Guide
The annually updated *Definitive(ly) Good Guide to Restaurants* is a pocket-sized gourmet bible for many island residents, reflecting the opinions of restaurant-goers rather than critics. It is available from local bookshops, and you can recoup the cost by using discount vouchers at the back. The maps are also very useful.

2 When to Eat
The Maltese tend to eat their main meal at lunchtime, and they like to eat a lot; there are often five or six courses, and lunch may last for several hours, especially at weekends. Eating times are similar to those of northern Europe: lunch about 1pm and dinner about 7pm.

3 Restaurant Opening Hours
Most restaurants in major resorts open for lunch and dinner in the high season, but have reduced hours (or even close altogether) in winter. Valletta is different: it virtually shuts down in the evening, and many restaurants are open for lunch only. Restaurants in the country and smaller villages are also likely to close in the evenings.

4 Self-catering and Picnicking
There is plenty of self-catering accommodation in Malta, from budget apartments in resorts to beautifully restored Gozitan farmhouses and historic apartments in Valletta. The best food is often the simplest – heavenly bread, plump tomatoes and peppered Gozitan cheese that are perfect for picnics.

5 What to Buy
Malta has long been known for its jewellery, particularly silver filigree. Maltese crosses are also popular buys. Woollen jumpers and rugs from Gozo are expensive but make great souvenirs. The islands are also famous for lace, but most of what you'll see is machine-made. Handmade lace is harder to find and more expensive, but beautiful. Colourful hand-blown glass from Mdina and local ceramics also make attractive souvenirs.

6 Maltese Craft Villages
Malta and Gozo both have craft villages *(see pp88, 102)*, where you'll find all the traditional local crafts and can buy souvenirs at reasonable prices. Both craft villages also give demonstrations.

7 Shopping Hours
Smaller shops usually open from 9am to 1 or 2pm and from 3 or 4pm to about 7pm. Many close for a half-day once a week, and many also open on Saturday afternoons. Department stores, chain stores and bigger shops stay open at midday, and those in big towns (such as Sliema) often until 8 or 9pm. Virtually nothing is open on Sundays, even in big resorts.

8 Markets
Valletta has a daily market for clothes, CDs, souvenirs, etc, and a big Sunday flea market. On the quays at Marsaxlokk there's a tourist market, with a colourful and pungent fish market on Sundays. For the freshest fruit and vegetables, buy from produce vans to be found parked on corners.

9 Low-season Bargains
April and October are usually cheaper than July to September, but for the best bargains visit Malta in winter. Accommodation prices plummet, and fantastic bargains can be had by shopping around.

10 Websites for Hotel Discounts
Tour-operators block-book many hotels, and may be cheapest overall. The tourism authority doesn't offer a hotel-booking service, but its website has a hotel-search facility. Several websites offer discounts on Maltese hotels – but double-check with the hotel's own website to make sure it isn't offering even better deals. ✆ www.mta.com.mt • www.hotelclub.net • www.ANOther.com

Many of Valletta's restaurants don't open in the evenings; call in advance.

Left **Unattended valuables** Centre **Sunbathers** Right **Parking in Valletta**

Things to Avoid

1 Hunters
Malta has more than 16,000 hunters and trappers in a population of under 400,000. They kill 2–3 million birds a year, including endangered species protected under European and Maltese law. Gun-toting hunters regularly haunt some of the most beautiful and unspoilt corners (ignoring hunting seasons and protected areas), so be wary while out hiking. Contact the conservation group BirdLife Malta for more information.
🕭 *www.birdlifemalta.org*

2 Driving
Malta has the highest road-accident rate in Europe. It's best to avoid driving altogether – especially in Valletta, where it can be extremely difficult to park – but if you do get behind the wheel, remember that Maltese drivers don't believe in speed restrictions, using indicators or giving way. Expect any courtesy you show to be treated as a sign of weakness. Be especially wary of buses; their drivers treat other road-users as invisible.

3 Visiting in August
Malta's population explodes in August, when nearly 200,000 visitors arrive. Rooms are scarce and expensive, beaches are crammed, and the heat excessive. On the plus side, the beach-holiday requisites of sun, sea and sand are all at their peak and it's a good season for *festas*.

4 Leaving Valuables in a Car
Malta has less crime than most other parts of Europe, but thieves have begun to target cars parked in rural areas. So take all valuables with you and open the glove compartment to show there is nothing of value.

5 Sleeping in Paċeville
Paċeville is Malta's party capital, with dozens of bars crammed in a few small streets. It's popular with teenagers, who hang out on the streets until the small hours. The hotels in the area are best left to night-owls.

6 Relying on Opening Times
In Malta, as in much of the Mediterranean, time is a fluid concept. Don't expect posted opening hours in museums, shops or restaurants to be exact. Everything may close without notice – or stay open later than you expect. If you are particularly keen to see a museum or eat at a certain restaurant, it's wise to phone ahead.

7 Excessive Sun
Northern European visitors are easy to spot in Malta: they are usually shiny and scarlet. The Maltese themselves are avid, but sensible, sun-worshippers. Follow their example and avoid sun-bathing between noon and 4pm, always use a good sunscreen, and drink plenty of water.

8 Smoking
Smoking is banned in all public places, including restaurants, bars, shops, public areas in hotels, and the airport. Many restaurants and bars have outdoor smoking areas, and a few larger establishments have smoking sections.

9 Wasting Water
Water is scarce. Try to save it by taking showers rather than baths, turning the tap off while brushing teeth or shaving, and asking your hotel to change sheets and towels less often.

10 Unscrupulous Taxi-drivers
Some taxi-drivers try to charge whatever they think passengers will pay, rather than the official rates posted near taxi ranks. Taxis should use their meters, but almost never do, so agree the fare in advance. There are no supplements for luggage, for extra passengers (up to four), or for the day or time of the journey. Contact the Malta Transport Authority with complaints. 🕭 *Sa Maison Road, Floriana • 2560 8000 • www. maltatransport.com*

Left **Hilton Malta, St Julian's** Centre **Le Méridien Phoenicia, Floriana** Right **Ta' Ċenċ, Sannat (Gozo)**

Luxury Retreats

Corinthia Palace Hotel, San Anton

An elegant refuge set in beautifully landscaped gardens in quiet, chichi San Anton, the Palace pampers guests with indoor and outdoor pools, a lavish spa, a gym, and three restaurants. A minibus shuttles guests to a private beach in St George's Bay. ◈ *Pjazza de Paule • Map C4 • 2144 0301 • €€€€€ • www. corinthiahotels.com*

Grand Hotel Mercure Selmun Palace, Mellieħa

The nucleus is a converted 18th-century castle set on an unspoilt promontory, quiet yet close enough to Mellieħa for the nightlife. Sports facilities include a gym, indoor and outdoor pools, tennis, and archery. The two restaurants have poolside terraces, and there's live entertainment. ◈ *Selmun, nr Mellieħa • Map B2 • 2152 1040 • €€€€€ • www.mercure.com*

Radisson SAS Golden Sands Resort and Spa, Golden Bay

Huge and glossy, this newly built resort hotel overlooks one of Malta's best beaches and offers every five-star luxury. It has extensive sports facilities, a large spa, and a private sandy beach. It is also secluded, the only hotel in the bay. ◈ *Map A3 • 2356 1000 • €€€€€ • www.radissonsas.com*

Fortina Spa Resort, Sliema

Enjoy your own en-suite spa – plus, in some rooms, a private roof terrace and seawater pool, and/or a view of Valletta. This vast complex includes fitness and diving centres, and eight restaurants. ◈ *Tigne Seafront • Map R3 • 2346 0000 • €€€€€ • www. hotelfortina.com*

Le Méridien Phoenicia, Floriana

Formal afternoon tea is still served at this 1920s *grande dame*. The hotel is set in seven acres of landscaped gardens just outside Valletta's city walls, and many rooms enjoy wonderful harbour views. There's an outdoor pool. ◈ *The Mall • Map G3 • 2122 5241 • €€€€€ • www.malta.lemeridien.com*

Radisson SAS Bay Point Resort, St Julian's

This vast resort hotel has it all: elegant boutiques, diving and watersports centres, business facilities and a whole range of restaurants and bars. ◈ *St George's Bay • Map D3 • 2137 4894 • €€€€€ • www.radissonsas.com*

Hilton Malta, St Julian's

Part of a new development beside Spinola Bay, the Hilton offers every luxury, from a private beach club to its own marina. There are pools, a gym, a dance studio, tennis and squash courts, and various health and beauty treatments. ◈ *Portomaso • Map P1 • 2138 3383 • €€€€€ • www.hilton.com*

Le Méridien St Julian's

This stylish new hotel is set in a 19th-century villa overlooking Balluta Bay. Amenities include the spectacular Lotus Spa in a glass atrium and several restaurants under an award-winning chef. ◈ *39 Triq Il-Kbira, Balluta Bay • Map P2 • 2311 0000 • €€€€€ • www.malta. lemeridien.com*

Ta' Ċenċ, Sannat, Gozo

The romantic, village-style Ta' Ċenċ's rooms and apartments are built from creamy limestone; the circular "trullos" are most desirable. There's a spa, gardens, pools, gym and outdoor restaurant. A shuttle bus serves a private beach. ◈ *Map E2 • 2155 6819 • €€€€€ • www.vjborg.com/tacenc*

Kempinski St Lawrenz Resort & Spa, Gozo

Built of creamy stone and set in subtropical gardens, this is a stylish and tranquil retreat. It is one of Europe's finest spas, and offers Ayurveda and other different but complementary health and beauty treatments. ◈ *Triq Ir-Rokon • Map D1 • 2211 0000 • €€€€€ • www.kempinski-gozo.com*

  The standard of accommodation in Malta has improved dramatically over the last few years, with many new luxury hotels.

Dar Ta' Zeppi

Price Categories

For a standard, double room per night (with breakfast if included), taxes and extra charges.

€	under 15 Lm/€35
€€	15–30 Lm/€35–70
€€€	30–45 Lm/€70–105
€€€€	45–60 Lm/€105–140
€€€€€	over 60 Lm/€140

TOP 10 Characterful Places to Stay

1 Hotel Juliani, St Julian's

Malta's first boutique hotel is still the epitome of urban cool, furnished in a slick mix of antique and contemporary. Its restaurants and bars are the most fashionable on buzzy Spinola Bay. The tiny rooftop pool and deck offer fabulous views. 🕲 12 Triq San Ġorġ • Map P1 • 2138 8000 • €€€€ • www.hoteljuliani.com

2 Xara Palace, Mdina

Housed in a magnificent palace within the walls of the "Silent City", this is the perfect spot to soak up Mdina's atmosphere when the tour groups have left. Its restaurants, particularly De Mondion (see p89), are superb, and it has a luxurious spa. 🕲 Misraħ Il-Kunsill • Map C4 • 2145 0560 • €€€€€ • www.xarapalace.com.mt

3 Hotel Castille, Valletta

A welcoming hotel in a rosy-pink Baroque palace. There's a great rooftop restaurant with views to the Grand Harbour and a cosy, vaulted pizza restaurant in the cellar. 🕲 Misraħ Kastilja • Map H3 • 2124 3677 • €€€ • www.hotelcastillemalta.com

4 Hotel Osborne, Valletta

The rather creaky and old-fashioned Osborne makes a refreshing change from Malta's many anonymous concrete boxes. Rooms are basic, but the service excellent and the location perfect for sightseeing in Valletta. You can eat in but there are better options close-by. 🕲 50 Triq Nofs In-Nhar • Map H2 • 2124 3656 • €€ • www.osbornehotel.com

5 Valletta G-House, Valletta

An unusual and charming apartment in a beautiful historic building. It is stylishly decorated with objets d'art, paintings and antiques, but has 21st-century gadgets. Guests are met at the airport, and a welcome basket awaits. It can't be beaten for romance. 🕲 Triq Il-Fran • Map J2 • +44 (0) 781 39 888 27 • €€ • www.vallettahouse.com

6 Imperial Hotel, Sliema

The Imperial retains 19th-century details, including a sweeping staircase that once featured in a James Bond movie. The lobby has a glittering chandelier and glossy marble, but the rooms are rather bland. There's a garden with stone arches and a large outdoor pool. 🕲 Triq Rodolfu • Map Q3 • 2134 4093 • €€€€ • www.imperialhotelmalta.com

7 Maritim Antoine Hotel & Spa, Mellieħa

This peach-painted hotel has a commanding view, and is one of the most attractive in Mellieħa. One pool is set in lush gardens, another on the roof, and a third indoors. 🕲 Triq Borġ Olivier • Map B2 • 2152 0923 • €€€€ • www.maritim.com.mt

8 Ta' Pietru, Għarb, Gozo

Accommodation with charm is hard to find in Malta, but the stone farmhouses of Gozo are a delightful exception. This one is particularly attractive, and there's an outdoor pool and sun terrace. 🕲 Triq It-Trux • Map D1 • 9947 2609 • €€€

9 Dar Ta' Zeppi, Qala, Gozo

There are just two stylish, high-ceilinged rooms in this beautiful house, each big enough for a family. Tanja, a superb cook, prepares spectacular Mediterranean cuisine in the evenings, while Victor regales guests with stories. There's a lovely pool in the garden. 🕲 39 28th April 1688 Street • Map F2 • 2155 5051 • €€€ • www.dartazeppi.com

10 Xagħra Lodge, Xagħra, Gozo

A British couple run this cosy guesthouse, with quintessentially English decor, in a sleepy village. It has a honeymoon suite with four-poster bed, family rooms and a pool in the garden. 🕲 Triq Dun George Preca • Map E1 • 2156 2362 • €€ • www.gozo.com/xaghralodge

In Jan 2008, Malta abandons the Maltese lira (Lm) and adopts the euro (€); the price categories above refer to both currencies.

Left **Gillieru Harbour** Right **Hotel Comino**

🏆10 Seaside Charmers

1 Hotel Comino, Comino

The only accommodation on Comino, this pink-painted hotel overlooks a little bay and private beach, so you can enjoy the island's peace once the day-trippers have left. The rooms are simple, but there are good sports facilities. Prices are for half-board. 🏵 *San Niklaw Bay • Map F2 • 2152 9821 • Open Apr–Oct • €€€€ • www.cominohotel.com*

2 Grand Hotel, Mġarr, Gozo

From its commanding position on the hill above Mġarr Harbour, the Grand gives magnificent views of the port and its brightly painted fishing boats. The prettiest rooms have private balconies that overlook the port. The restaurant is one of the best on Gozo, and has a breezy summer terrace. 🏵 *Triq Sant' Anton, Għajnsielem • Map F2 • 2156 3840 • €€€€ • www.grandhotelmalta.com*

3 St Patrick's Hotel, Xlendi, Gozo

A smart, whitewashed hotel right by the sea. The rooms have rather dated furnishings but the best have a Jacuzzi and a terrace overlooking the magnificent natural bay. There's a small rooftop pool with sun deck and a popular seafront bar. 🏵 *Xatt Ix-Xlendi • Map D2 • 2156 2951 • €€€€ • www.vjborg.com/stpatricks*

4 San Andrea, Xlendi, Gozo

Modern, but traditional in style, with archways and iron grilles. It's cosy and intimate, with 28 pretty rooms. There are great views from the roof deck but no pool. The location can't be beaten. 🏵 *St Xlendi Promenade • Map D2 • 2156 5555 • €€€ • www.hotelsanandrea.com*

5 Hostel Maria-Giovanna, Marsalforn, Gozo

A delightful budget option, this traditional stone townhouse has just five guest rooms, with and without en-suite facilities. Marsalforn's restaurants and nightlife are on the doorstep, but it's also easy to get away into the country. 🏵 *Marsalforn Bay • Map E1 • 2155 3630 • € • www.gozohostels.com*

6 Golden Sun Aparthotel, Marsaxlokk

The only place to stay in quiet Marsaxlokk, this offers very basic self-catering apartments and hotel rooms. Not all of the latter have en-suite facilities, but some are suitable for families. 🏵 *Triq Il-Kajjik • Map F5 • 2165 1762 • €€ • www.goldensunhotelmalta.com*

7 Waterfront Hotel, Sliema

A shiny, modern seafront hotel with views across to Valletta. There's a small rooftop pool with deck, and a good restaurant overlooking the bay. You can order picnic lunches. 🏵 *Triq Ix-Xatt, Gzira • Map Q3 • 2133 3434 • €€€ • www.waterfrontmalta.com.mt*

8 Victoria Hotel, Sliema

The recently refurbished Victoria has an elegant interior evoking a 19th-century gentlemen's club. It has a courtyard pool and small sun terrace. The same management runs the luxurious Palazzo Capua. 🏵 *Triq Gorġ Borg Olivier • Map P2 • 2133 4711 • €€€€ • www.victoriahotel.com*

9 Corinthia Jerma Palace, Marsaskala

The best of Marsaskala's rather ordinary bunch, this huge resort stands on a promontory. Its amenities include watersports, a health club with gym and sauna, live entertainment and a children's pool and club. 🏵 *Dawret It-Torri • Map F5 • 2163 3222 • €€€€ • www.corinthiahotels.com*

10 Gillieru Harbour, St Paul's Bay

A modest, simple, and friendly hotel close to the harbour. Some rooms have splendid views. There's an excellent restaurant, a small pool, and a breezy sun terrace. Good value. 🏵 *Church Square • Map C3 • 2157 2723 • €€ • gillieru@vol.net.mt*

Cornucopia Hotel

🔟 Family-friendly Hotels

1 Westin Dragonara Resort, St Julian's

One of Malta's most lavish resorts, the vast Dragonara has something for all, including health and beauty facilities, a private beach, and all-year family entertainment – from sports tournaments to painting lessons. There are colouring books in the restaurants and electrical outlet covers in bedrooms. ⊗ Triq Dragonara • Map D3 • 2138 1000 • €€€€€ • www.westinmalta.com

2 Bay Street Hotel, St Julian's

Ideal for families with teenagers, this is part of a large shopping and entertainment complex, near the buzzy nightlife of Paċeville. Family rooms and studio apartments with small kitchenettes are available. There's a rooftop pool and a small spa and beauty centre. ⊗ Bay Street Complex, St George's Bay • Map D3 • 2138 4421 • €€€€ • baystreet.com.mt/hotel

3 Dolmen Resort Hotel, St Paul's Bay

This smart establishment is named after the megalithic remains in the gardens. There are good-value family rooms and a summer Kids' Club with all kinds of activities. Parents can relax at the spa and there are four pools set in lush gardens. ⊗ Qawra • Map C3 • 2355 2355 • €€€€ • www.dolmen.com.mt

4 Ramla Bay Resort, Marfa

A newly refurbished hotel on a small bay, this is good for families who want a quiet break. There are indoor and outdoor pools, a safe sandy beach, and good watersports facilities, but the nearest towns are a bus-ride away. ⊗ Triq il-Marfa • Map A2 • 2281 2281 • €€€ • www.ramlabayresort.com

5 Hotel Riu Seabank & Spa, Mellieħa

Just across the road from this modern hotel is probably the best sandy beach in Malta, with watersports, lidos, bars and cafés. The hotel has a jungle-themed restaurant, outdoor pool, gym and sauna, and bowling alley. ⊗ Triq il-Marfa • Map B2 • 2152 1460 • €€€€ • www.seabankhotel.com

6 Solana Hotel, Mellieħa

The modern, traditional-style Solana has indoor and outdoor pools, a games room, and weekly summer barbecues. Its diving school offers special children's courses. ⊗ Triq Ġorġ Borġ Olivier • Map B2 • 2152 2209 • €€€ • www.solanahotel.com

7 Paradise Bay Resort Hotel, Ċirkewwa

This large, pink-painted hotel near the Malta-Gozo ferry terminal has its own beach. Its modest rooms are good value, and there are child-friendly restaurants, four pools, a games room, and summer barbecues. ⊗ Paradise Bay • Map A2 • 2152 1166 • €€€ • www.paradise-bay.com

8 Cornucopia, Xagħra, Gozo

A converted farmhouse forms the heart of this complex, set around a flower-filled courtyard with a pool; there's also a children's pool. It has family rooms and suites. ⊗ Triq Gnien Imrik • Map E1 • 2155 6486 • €€€ • www.vjborg.com/cornucopia

9 Hotel Serena Beach Club, Xlendi, Gozo

A large, modern complex overlooking Xlendi Bay, this has a panoramic glass lift down to the beach. There's a rooftop pool, tiny fitness room, and small supermarket. Hotel rooms and self-catering apartments are available. ⊗ Triq Punici • Map D2 • 2155 3719 • €€€€ • www.serena.com.mt

10 Carolina Hotel, Buġibba

Near the seafront and busy heart of Buġibba, the Carolina has indoor and outdoor pools, children's pool and games room, and rooftop bar. There are both hotel rooms and self-catering apartments. Karaoke nights and other events are organized in summer. ⊗ Triq San Anton • Map C3 • 2157 1534 • €€ • www.carolinahotel.com.mt

In Jan 2008, Malta abandons the Maltese lira (Lm) and adopts the euro (€); the price categories above refer to both currencies.

Left **Mariblu Guesthouse** Middle **Asti Guesthouse** Right **British Hotel restaurant balcony**

TOP 10 Budget Hotels and Guesthouses

1 Villa Rosa, St Julian's
This rambling villa on the St George's Bay seafront has basic accommodation for groups and families. Rooms sleep up to six, and there's a pool and sun terrace with lovely views. ◊ *St George's Bay • Map D3 • 2134 2707 • € • villarosa@maltanet.net*

2 The Gardens, Rabat/Victoria, Gozo
Gozo's capital has little accommodation of any kind, but this guesthouse on the outskirts is well sited for exploring the island. It's an informal set-up, with five rooms sharing two bathrooms, the kitchen, and a roof garden. ◊ *Kercem Road • Map D2 • 2155 3723 • € • www.casalgoholidays.com*

3 Soleado Guesthouse, Sliema
This friendly, family-run guesthouse is in the heart of Sliema's nightlife and shopping area, so it's a good choice for young travellers on a budget. It offers rooms with or without en-suite facilities. ◊ *Triq Ghar Id-Dud • Map R3 • 2133 4415 • € • www.soleadomalta.com*

4 British Hotel, Valletta
The gloomy, 1970s-style lobby belies the bright rooms upstairs. Most have en-suite bathrooms, and the best, fine views of the Grand Harbour. (A sixth-floor room with a sea view costs extra.) Give the hotel restaurant a miss, but head for the roof bar at sunset. ◊ *40 Triq Il-Batterija • Map J3 • 2122 4730 • €€ • www.britishhotel.com*

5 Asti Guesthouse, Valletta
An appealing guesthouse in an old convent built of creamy limestone, this is an ideal choice in the heart of the capital. There are just eight rooms, so book early. Although it has no restaurant, there are several options close by. ◊ *18 Triq Sant' Orsla • Map J3 • 2123 9506 • €*

6 Point de Vue, Rabat (Malta)
Book ahead for rooms in this recently refurbished guesthouse just outside the main gate to the "Silent City". ◊ *2/7 Is-Saqqajja • Map C4 • 2145 4117 • €€*

7 Lantern Guesthouse, Marsalforn, Gozo
This is one of the most appealing budget options in Marsalforn, offering simple en-suite rooms and basic apartments – good value for families or groups. There is a small fee for air conditioning, but the rooms have fans. Downstairs the Lantern has its own inexpensive restaurant and pizzeria. ◊ *Triq Qbajjar • Map E1 • 2156 2365 • €€ • www.gozo.com/lantern*

8 Mariblu Guesthouse, Xewkija, Gozo
This is a friendly, family-run guesthouse in a sleepy Gozitan village famous for its parish church *(see p39)*. The rooms, all with en-suite bathrooms, are above the Mariblu restaurant in the village centre. The owners also rent out villas and farmhouses. ◊ *Mġarr Road • Map E2 • 2155 1315 • €€ • www.mariblugozo.com*

9 Primera Hotel, Buġibba
Modern and functional, the Primera Hotel has a good central location and reasonable facilities for the price. There are indoor and outdoor pools, a kids' paddling pool, and a rooftop terrace for sunbathing. Rooms are plain, but equipped with air-conditioning and satellite TV. ◊ *Pioneer Rd • Map C3 • 2157 3880 • €€ • www.primera.com*

10 Splendid Guesthouse, Mellieħa
Pristine rooms (each with a shower or full en-suite facilities), a buzzy little bar and restaurant, a small sun terrace and charming owners make this the best budget deal in Mellieħa. The beach is a short bus-ride away, but shops and nightlife are close by. ◊ *Triq Kappillan Magri • Map B3 • 2152 0552 • €€ • www.splendidmalta.com*

Many of Gozo's traditional farmhouses have been restored and are rented to visitors as self-catering accommodation.

Comino Hotel Bungalows

Price Categories

For a standard, double room per night (with breakfast if included), taxes and extra charges.

€	under 15 Lm/€35
€€	15–30 Lm/€35–70
€€€	30–45 Lm/€70–105
€€€€	45–60 Lm/€105–140
€€€€€	over 60 Lm/€140

Self-catering Accommodation

1 Comino Hotel Bungalows

Neat rows of pink- and peach-painted bungalows overlook Comino's prettiest beach. They are linked via a panoramic, cliffside path to Hotel Comino (see p114), whose sports facilities and private beach they share. ✪ Santa Marija Bay • Map F1 • 2152 9821 • Open Apr–Oct • €€€€ • www.cominohotel.com

2 Gozo Prestige Holidays, Għarb

This reliable local business offers 16 magnificent Gozitan farmhouses for rent, all in idyllic locations near some of Gozo's prettiest villages. They are furnished in traditional rustic style and boast pools with Jacuzzis, barbecue areas, fully equipped kitchens, and multilingual TV. ✪ Triq San Pietru • 2155 1627 • €€€€

3 Howard Johnson Mediterranean Hotel & Suites, St Paul's Bay

A large complex with wonderful views, this offers accommodation ranging from regular hotel rooms to studios and one-, two-, and three-bedroom apartments with kitchenettes. There is a restaurant, bar and small rooftop pool, and the pretty fishermen's harbour is a short walk away. ✪ Triq Buġibba • Map C3 • 21571118 • €€€ • www.hojomed.com.mt

4 Mellieħa Holiday Centre

This large Danish-run tourist village sits just behind Mellieħa Bay. Its tastefully designed limestone bungalows and studios are set in gardens. The facilities include bars and restaurants, two pools (one for children), a tennis court, mini-golf, and a games room. ✪ Għadira Bay • Map B3 • 2289 3000 • €€€ • www.melliehaholidaycentre.com

5 Gozo Farmhouses, Għajnsielem

Beautiful farmhouses across Gozo have been restored using traditional techniques, and furnished luxuriously. Some boast antique four-poster beds and Jacuzzis; all have private pools. Food packs can be provided, or even a private chef to prepare local dishes. ✪ 3 Mġarr Road • 2156 1280 • €€€ • www.gozofarmhouses.com

6 Holiday Malta

This locally based online agency can organize self-catering apartments, farmhouses, and villas. It's particularly good for areas with few hotels or guesthouses, and also has characterful Valetta accommodation. ✪ €€€ • www.holiday-malta.com

7 Valletta Studios

Quaint and unusual studio apartments with views of the Grand Harbour. One boasts an original wood-panelled box gallery, typical of Valletta's architecture. Extras such as CD- and DVD-players make them feel like a home-from-home. ✪ 63 Triq Il-Batterija • Map J3 • 2125 1748 • €€ • www.vallettastudios.com

8 Dar Ta' Zeppi, Qala, Gozo

This charming, artistically restored house has two spacious rooms, each big enough for a family and with kitchenettes. Prices include at least breakfast, but you can cook other meals yourself. ✪ 39 28th April 1688 St • Map F1 • 2155 5051 • €€€ • www.dartazeppi.com

9 Villa Renters

This large, UK-based web company has a wide range of farmhouses and villas for rent. You then contact the owners direct and pay by credit card. ✪ www.villa-holiday.co.uk

10 Pebbles Aparthotel, Sliema

A cheerful family-run option on the seafront, Pebbles offers functionally furnished apartments with kitchenettes. In summer, it also runs the Pebbles Lido, 1 km (half a mile) away, with sun-loungers, two seawater pools, a children's pool, and a watersports centre with everything from banana-boat rides to yacht charter. ✪ 88-89 Triq Ix-Xatt • Map Q3 • 2131 1889 • €€ • www.maltaaparthotels.com

In Jan 2008, Malta abandons the Maltese lira (Lm) and adopts the euro (€); the price categories above refer to both currencies.

General Index

General Index

Acknowledgements

The Author
Mary-Ann Gallagher is a widely experienced travel writer, now based in Barcelona. She has written and contributed to several Dorling Kindersley titles including *Top 10 Costa Blanca* and *RealCity Barcelona*, as well as guides for other publishers to Crete, Vienna and many other destinations.

The author wishes to thank all in Malta who provided her with invaluable help, among them: Shirley Psaila at the Maltese tourist office; Pierre Cassar at Heritage Malta; Mario Farrugia at Fondazzjoni Wirt Artna; Jo Balzan at St John's Co-Cathedral; Stephen Cini at Gozo's Museum of Archaeology; Tanya van Poucke and her delightful family at Dar ta Zeppi; Freddie at the Animal Sanctuary; and Lucia Mizzi.

Produced by Coppermill Books, 55 Salop Road London E17 7HS

Editorial Director Chris Barstow

Designer Ian Midson
Copy Editor Michael Wright
Proofreader Antony Mason
Fact-checker Christine Debono
Indexer Hilary Bird

Main Photographer Antony Souter
Additional Photography Rough Guides/Eddie Gerald
Illustrator Chapel Design & Marketing
Maps Dominic Beddow and Simonetta Giori at Draughtsman Maps

FOR DORLING KINDERSLEY
Publisher Douglas Amrine
Publishing Manager Vivien Antwi
Design Manager Karen Constanti
Senior Cartographic Editor Casper Morris
DTP Designer Natasha Lu
Production Controller Linda Dare

Picture Credits
Placement Key: t-top; tl-top left; tlc-top left centre; tc-top centre; tr-top right; cla-centre left above; ca-centre above; cra-centre right above; cl-centre left; c-centre; cr-centre right; clb-centre left below; cb-centre below; crb-centre right below; bl-bottom left, b-bottom; bc-bottom centre; bcl-bottom centre left; br-bottom right; d-detail.

Every effort has been made to trace the copyright holders and we apologize in advance for any unintentional omissions. We would be pleased to insert the appropriate acknowledgments in any subsequent edition of this publication.

The publishers would like to thank the following individuals, companies and picture libraries for their kind permission to reproduce their photographs.

BRIDGEMAN ART LIBRARY:
Private Collection 13clb, Bibliothèque Nationale, Paris 13br
DANIEL CILIA: 7tr, 22cla, 22c, 22br, 23tr, 23ca, 23bc, 93c
GETTY IMAGES/HULTON ARCHIVE: 33cl
MALTA TOURISM AUTHORITY: 48tl, 48tr, 48bl, 49tr, 49br

All other images are © Dorling Kindersley. For further information see *www.dkimages.com*

Phrase Book

Phrase Book *(side margin)*

Virtually everyone in Malta is bilingual and speaks Malti and English with equal fluency. Locals don't expect visitors to be able to speak Malti, but appreciate efforts to say a few words in their language. The written Maltese language uses some unsual characters – some letters are crossed and others have a dot. This means that some place names, for example, can be hard to pronounce without a little help.

Maltese Pronunciation Key

ċ – as ch in church
e – as in get
g – (hard) as in good
g - (soft) as in gentle
h – usually silent
ħ – as "h" in hand
i – (long) as "ee", e.g. see
j – as "y" in yacht
gh – usually silent
q – silent
x – (soft) as "sh", e.g. sheep
ż - (soft) as in zebra
z – as "ts", e.g. cats

In an Emergency

Get the police	**Sejjah pulizija**	sey-yah pul-its-iya
Danger	**Periklu**	peh-ree-klu
Fire	**Nar**	nahr
Get a doctor	**Sejjah tabib**	sey-yah tab-eeb
Go away	**Mur 'l hemm**	moor lemm
Help	**Ajjut**	ay-ut
I'm lost	**Intlift**	int-li-ft
Police	**Pulizija**	poo-lee-tsee-yah

Communication Essentials

Yes	**Iva**	ee-vah
No	**Le**	leh
Please	**Jekk joghgbok**	yek yoj-bok
Thank you	**Grazzi**	grah-tsi
Thank you very much	**Grazzi hafna**	grah-tsi ah-fnah
You're welcome	**M'hemmx mn'hiex**	memsh mneesh
Good morning	**Bongu**	bohn-joo
Good evening	**Bonswa**	bohn-swar
Good night	**Il-lejl it-tajjeb**	ill-ale ee-tay-eb
Good-bye	**Sahha**	sah-ha
So long	**Caw**	chow
See you later	**Narak iktar tard**	nah-rak ik-tah tard
Sorry!	**Skuzani!**	skoo-zah-nee

Where?	**Fejn?**	fayn
How?	**Kif?**	keef
When?	**Meta?**	meh-tah
What?	**X'hini?**	sheen-eey
Why?	**Ghaliex?**	ah-leesh
Who?	**Min?**	meen
Which?	**Liema?**	lee-mah

Useful Phrases

Pleased to meet you	**Ghandi pjacir**	ahn-dee pee-yach-eer
How are you?	**Kif inti?**	keef een-tee
Very well, thanks	**Tajjeb, grazzi**	tay-eb, grah-zee
And you?	**hafna U inti?**	haf-nah oo een-tee
I beg your pardon?	**Skuzi?**	skoo-zee
Excuse me	**Skuzi!**	skoo-zee
Where is...?	**Fejn hu...?**	fayn yoo
Where are...?	**Fejn huma?**	fayn yoo-mah
Where can I find?	**Fejn nista insib?**	feyn nee-stah een-seeb
How long...?	**Kemm iddum?**	kehm ee-duhm
How much/many?	**Kemm...?**	kehm
How much is this?	**Kemm iqum dan/din?**	kehm ee-um dahn dan/deen
Do you speak English?	**Titkellem bl-Ingliz?**	teet-keh-luhm bul een-gleese
I understand	**Nifhem**	nee-fehm
I don't understand	**Ma nifhimx**	mah nee-fimsh
Can you help?	**Tista' tghinni?**	tis-tah tay-nee
I'd like	**Nixtieq**	nish-ti
We'd like	**Nixtiequ**	nish-ti-oo
I'm lost	**Intlift Il-Milied it-Tajjeb!**	eent-leeft eel mee-leed eet-tay-eb
Happy New Year!	**Is-Sena t-Tajba!**	iss-ehn-nah eet-tay-bah
Happy Easter!	**L-Ghid it-Tajjeb!**	layd eet tay-eb
Best Wishes!	**Xewqat Sbieh!**	shew-aht sbee
Congratulations!	**Nifrahlek!**	nee-frah-rah-lek
Good luck!	**Ix-Xorti t-Tajba!**	ish-shaw-tee eet-tay-bah

Numbers

0	**xejn**	shayn
1	**wiehed**	wee-ed
2	**tnejn**	tuh-nayn

3	**tlieta**	tuh-lee-tah
4	**erbgha**	ehr-bah
5	**hamsa**	ham-sah
6	**sitta**	see-tah
7	**sebgha**	seh-bah
8	**tmienja**	tuh-mee-nyah
9	**disgha**	dee-sah
10	**ghaxra**	ash-rah
11	**hdax**	huh-dash
12	**tnax**	tuh-nash
13	**tlettax**	tuh-leh-tash
14	**erbatax**	ehr-bah-tash
15	**hmistax**	huh-mee-stash
16	**sittax**	see-tash
17	**sbatax**	suh-bah-tash
18	**tmintax**	tuh-meen-tash
19	**dsatax**	tuh-tsa-tash
20	**ghoxrin**	oh-shreen
21	**wiehed u ghoxrin**	wee-ed oo oh-shreen
22	**tnejn u ghoxrin**	tneyn oo oh-shreen
30	**tletin**	tuh-leht-een
40	**erbghin**	er-beyn
50	**hamsin**	ham-seen
60	**sittin**	see-teen
70	**sebghin**	she-beyn
80	**tmenin**	tuh-men-een
90	**disghin**	dis-seyn
100	**mija**	mee-yah
1,000	**elf**	elf
1,000,000	**miljun**	meel-yun

Pronunciation of Place Names

Some places – for example, those with Italian names like Valletta and Vittoriosa – are pronounced just as they are spelt. But Maltese names can be tongue-twisters for visitors. Here are some of the trickier ones:

Birżebbuġa	beer-zay-boo-jah
Buġibba	boo-jee-bah
Ċirkewwa	cheer-keh-wah
Dwejra	dway-rah
Ġgantija	ja-gan-tee-yah
Gharb	ahrb
Ħaġar Qim	ha-jar-eem
Luqa	loo-ah
Marsaxlokk	marsah-shlock
Mdina	im-deena
Mellieħa	mell-ee-hah
Mġarr	im-jar
Msida	im-see-dah
Naxxar	nah-shar
Paċeville	pah-tchay-veel
Qawra	ow-rah

Siġġiewi	sij-ee-wee
Tarxien	tahr-shin
Xaghra	shah-rah
Xewkija	show-kee-jah
Xlendi	shlen-dee

Valletta Street Names

Most street signs are in Malti, but it's worth being familiar with their English equivalents; most shops and businesses use them, some maps are in English only – and you may simply find it easier to say South St than Triq Nofs In-Nhar. Here is a selective list:

Britannja, Triq	Brittania St
Girolamo Cassar, Triq	Girolamo Cassar St
Id-Dejqa, Triq	Strait St
Il-Batterija, Triq	Battery St
Il-Fontana, Triq	Fountain St
Il-Fran, Triq	Old Bakery St
Il-Mall	The Mall
Il-Mediterran, Triq	Mediterranean St
Il-Merkanti, Triq	Merchant's St
Il-Punent, Triq	West St
Ir-Repubblika, Misrah	Republic Sq
Ir-Repubblika, Triq	Republic St
It-Teatru L'Antik, Triq	Old Theatre St
Kastilja, Misrah	Castille Sq
L'4 Ta' Settembru, Misrah	4th September St
L'Arcisoof, Triq	Archbishop St
L'Assedju L-Kbir, Triq	Great Siege St
L'Ispar Il-Quadim, Triq	Old Hospital St
Lascaris, Triq	Lascaris St
L'Imithen, Triq	Windmill St
Marsamxett, Triq	Marsamxett St
Mattia Preti, Pjazza	Mattia Preti Sq
Melita, Triq	Melita St
Nelson, Triq	Nelson St
Nofs In-Nhar, Triq	South St
Papa Benedittu XV, Misrah	Pope Benedict XV St
Papa Piju V, Triq	Pope Pius V
San Bastian, Triq	St Sebastian St
San Duminku, Triq	St Dominic St
San Ġwann, Misrah	St John Sq
San Ġwann, Triq	St John St
San Kristofru, Triq	St Christoper St
San Marku, Triq	St Mark St
San Nikola, Triq	St Nicholas St
San Patrizju, Triq	St Patrick St
San Pawl, Triq	St Paul St
Sant' Anna, Triq	St Anna St
Sant' Ursula, Triq	St Ursula St
Santa Lucija, Triq	St Lucija St
Sarria, Triq	Sarria St
Zakkarija, Triq	Zachary St
Zekka, Triq	Old Mint St

Selected Map Indexes